"Within this book, Robert Leahy, a renowned world leader in our field, illuminates the complex burdens of this universal emotion of jealousy within a love relationship. He then points the way out of this tumultuous storm of thoughts and feelings by offering clear, specific, and practical steps. This is by far the best self-help book for people with jealousy that I have ever read."

—**Reid Wilson, PhD**, author of *Stopping the Noise in Your Head*

"Do you have a jealousy problem? Does it interfere with your relationship? Are you consumed with jealous thoughts and jealous feelings? Do you wish you could decrease your suffering? If so, you need this book! Robert Leahy clearly expresses why we feel jealous, he normalizes this intense experience, and he explains how our emotions and our thinking get highjacked. Then he details what to do. He teaches the reader how to detach from jealous thoughts and disengage from unhelpful behavior. He offers tools for coping with jealousy and various strategies to solve problems that it causes in relationships. *The Jealousy Cure* will help individuals who suffer from jealousy and those who are in relationships with jealous partners. As a stand-alone book or an accompaniment to therapy, *The Jealousy Cure* is very well written and quite interesting (even if you don't have a jealousy problem). Most of all, it provides essential skills for couples who need to improve their relationships."

—**Judith S. Beck, PhD**, president of the Beck Institute for Cognitive Behavior Therapy

"In *The Jealousy Cure*, Robert Leahy has provided the reader with a comprehensive understanding of jealousy.... Leahy, through interactive, fun exercises, helps the reader identify and understand their jealousy. Based on the tried-and-true principles of cognitive behavioral therapy (CBT), Leahy then equips the reader to address their jealousy so that problematic behaviors and tormenting thoughts and feelings can be reduced. This highly informative and valuable resource will be an essential resource to both those in clinical practice and individuals struggling with jealously."

> —**Leslie Sokol, PhD**, coauthor of *Think Confident, Be Confident*; *Think Confident, Be Confident for Teens*; and *The Think Confident, Be Confident Workbook for Teens*

"In his latest book, Robert Leahy—acclaimed psychologist and author of *The Worry Cure*—offers a creative and penetrating, yet hopeful, perspective on jealousy; one of the most misunderstood and highly destructive human emotions. Based on decades of psychotherapy experience and a unique adaptation of the cognitive behavioral approach to emotion, this well-researched, thought-provoking, and practical therapeutic manual provides valuable strategies that can liberate those inflicted with the self-defeating effects of pathological jealousy. Couples caught up in the jealousy vortex will discover wise counsel offered with sensitivity and compassion, making this a must-read for those seeking answers for tormented intimate partners."

> —**David A. Clark, PhD, LPsych**, professor emeritus at the University of New Brunswick, Canada; author of *The Anxious Thoughts Workbook*; and coauthor of *The Anxiety and Worry Workbook*

The
Jealousy
Cure

Learn to Trust,
Overcome Possessiveness &
Save Your Relationship

ROBERT L. LEAHY, PhD

New Harbinger Publications, Inc.

Publisher's Note

Distributed in Canada by Raincoast Books

Copyright © 2018 by Robert L. Leahy
      New Harbinger Publications, Inc.
      5674 Shattuck Avenue
      Oakland, CA 94609
      www.newharbinger.com

Adult Attachment Scale is copyright © 1996 by Nancy L. Collins. Adapted with permission of the American Psychiatric Association. N. L. Collins, "Working Models of Attachment: Implications for Explanation, Emotion, and Behavior," *Journal of Personality and Social Psychology* 71, no. 4 (1996): 810.

Cover design by Amy Shoup

Acquired by Ryan Buresh

Edited by Jennifer Holder

All Rights Reserved

Library of Congress Cataloging-in-Publication Data on file

20   19   18

10   9   8   7   6   5   4   3   2   1 First Printing

Contents

Foreword

Ever since Freud began to explore the psychological implications of Darwin's discoveries, we have been forced to recognize that evolution set us up with some rather unpleasant dark sides. The history of humanity can be seen as a constant struggle between our capacity for violence and our potential for compassion. At the root of our most basic motivations is the issue of the survival and reproduction of our genes. Interpersonal competition is also in that mix, whether for resources or access to sexual (reproductive) opportunities. Out of these central conflicts arise a range of motivational processes, from narcissistic and psychopathic self-focused competitiveness to tribalism, prejudice, envy, and—the subject of this book—jealousy.

In pioneering work over many years, Dr. Robert Leahy has sought to marry an in-depth understanding of the evolutionary and social origins of our darker sides with our capacity to become more mindful of them and, ultimately, to take responsibility for them. As we become more aware of what drives us, we can become more invested in holding ourselves accountable for our behavior. This is clearly one of the core aims of this exceptional and important book.

Dr. Leahy shows us clearly how jealousy overlaps with and differs from envy. *Envy* occurs when we feel somebody or some group has more than we do, and we want what they have. Hostile forms of envy can lead us to destroy what others have, while beneficent forms of envy can lead us to imitate others and strive to become better. *Jealousy*, on the other hand, involves the competition among three or more people for the attention and positive dispositions of at least one of them. It is typically linked to sexual relationships, but not always so. Jealousy and envy overlap in their tendency to motivate hostile behavior toward their object, even to the point of wanting to harm and destroy others—hence the famous vow, "If I can't have it, nobody will."

The roots of jealousy can be seen in many other species, particularly in the behaviors called *mate guarding*, where individuals (mostly but not always males) try to both prevent others' access to those they are guarding and induce fear in those guarded. Indeed, the induction of fear is very common as a jealous tactic; in the Old Testament, at least, God was regarded as a jealous God capable of bringing untold miseries on those who would defect or disobey. The motto "Don't leave or else" underpins the threats of the jealous one.

It's not difficult to see that jealousy can be one of the greatest destroyers of compassionate relations; in the place of love, jealousy instills anger. Jealousy can power all kinds of relational conflicts, from passive-aggression all the way through to domestic violence and murder. Jealousy often sits behind stalking behavior, and it can motivate vengeance when the object of one's desires chooses another. In the end, jealousy is often the thing that drives away the person one most desires. And like many emotions in the anger family, jealousy also has a habit of justifying itself.

In *The Jealousy Cure*, Dr. Leahy brings his considerable experience as a clinician to this oft-neglected personal and relational tragedy. He provides deep insights into jealousy's source as well as what we can do about it. If you suffer from problems of jealousy, this book will help you recognize that you are far from alone, that you are experiencing the urges and pain of jealousy precisely because the human brain—your brain—has made it possible.

Dr. Leahy addresses with great sensitivity not only those who suffer from jealousy but also those who are on the receiving end.

Tragically, just as those who experience jealousy perpetrate hostile behaviors, those on the receiving end often feel ashamed of what is happening. They may try to hide the reality, even from themselves, and not reach out for help. Indeed, many victims of jealous undermining or violence can be too ashamed and frightened to acknowledge the kind of relationship they are caught in. This book may help you to see whether you are a victim of a jealous relationship, and may help you determine whether you might benefit from professional help.

The Jealousy Cure is immensely valuable for the clarity of its insights into the nature and patterns of jealousy. Especially important is the guidance on our capacity to release ourselves from shame over our experiences with jealousy. Being honest with ourselves is an important first step in taking responsibility for our behavior. We can't always stop what arises in our mind, but we can take responsibility for our actions and their consequences. Ultimately, we are short-lived, biologically determined beings— from the day we are born to the day we die, our urges and desires follow the dictates of a mind that evolved over millions of years. And even when our genes push us to grasp and control those we love, ultimately, it is in letting go of those urges that we can finally find peace and connection.

This is a deeply insightful and important book that will help you understand your jealousy and find its antidotes. You'll learn how to be honest with yourself and take the leap of courage needed to soothe your jealous mind. Dr. Leahy's writing is sensitive, accessible, and compassionate. Ultimately, conquering jealousy means freeing ourselves from an immensely painful and destructive human experience. Here is an outstanding step-by-step guide on that journey.

—Paul Gilbert, PhD, OBE

Introduction

Phyllis is usually a fun person to be around. Her laughter is infectious. She is intelligent, has a wonderful sense of humor, and shows a great deal of kindness toward almost everyone. She is attractive, creative, and has lots of friends. But Phyllis is plagued by jealous feelings about her boyfriend, Michael—feelings that overwhelm her at times—making her nauseated, anxious, and furious. She gets anxious when he is at parties and she worries about his friendship with his ex-girlfriend. When he has dinner with his ex-girlfriend, whom Michael describes as "only a friend," Phyllis goes into a rage. She thinks there is something wrong with her because she just can't get the jealousy out of her mind. "I think I am going crazy," she tells me as she looks down at the floor, avoiding eye contact.

Consider Steve. He didn't feel jealous when he first started dating Rachel, but now he does. He checks her Facebook page and tries to access her phone, looking for signs that she is losing interest in him. He keeps wondering: "Is she seeing someone else?" "Who is that guy who friended her on Facebook?" "Is she still looking?" Steve can't concentrate on work, is drinking more, and doesn't want to see his friends because he is so miserable. He tells me, "I really don't have a solid reason to think that Rachel is cheating, but don't know for sure. I can't stand the anxiety. I sometimes think that I would feel better if I just ended the relationship so I wouldn't have to worry anymore."

Almost everyone has felt jealousy at some point, or had jealous thoughts about a spouse, intimate partner, friend, sibling, or other family member. As you'll see in this book, jealousy is normal, as human as love and fear. It's a universal emotion that we find among people in different cultures, children, and even animals. We experience it because we feel connected to someone in a special way. So if that bond is at risk, we can feel threatened or insulted. We are seldom jealous about a superficial relationship, so jealousy may be a signal that someone matters. But when it takes over, like Phyllis and Steve we struggle to get it out of our minds and we may do things that we regret. Jealousy can create real problems for us.

I have written twenty-five books about psychology— addressing worry, anxiety, depression, and the difficulty of changing behavior—from the cognitive-behavioral therapy (CBT) approach. And I appreciate the wide range of gifted therapists who have also written books. So it struck me as odd that there was no book offering a CBT perspective to people struggling with jealousy in their lives. This was especially strange because jealousy involves many issues that we research and have effectively treated, including worry, rumination, self-criticism, anger, and conflict resolution. A book on it was overdue.

CBT has become the most highly valued treatment throughout the world for depression and anxiety, among many other problems that may cause you to struggle. It focuses on your current thoughts, behavior, and interactions with people to offer self-help tools so you can better cope with difficulties. In this book, I draw from a wide range of powerful techniques and conceptualizations that can help you cope with this often difficult and overwhelming emotion. My hope is to give you new tools that you can use today to put jealousy in perspective so that it does not control your life.

I have seen good people struggle with jealousy. They love their partners and want to trust and grow together. But they may escalate into uncontrollable anxiety and anger, which often lead to guilt and shame afterward. One woman cried with shame and fear because she was losing control and ruining her relationship.

A man hoped that the woman he was with would become a life partner, but his jealousy led him to interrogate her, accuse her, and stalk her on social media. Another man loved his wife and three children, but was so overwhelmed by jealous feelings that he thought it would be better to kill himself. Fortunately, he didn't and was able to rescue his marriage from the jealousy that had overtaken it.

This is a tragic emotion because jealousy comes from a combination of intense love and intense fear. The actions that result can jeopardize the very relationship that you want to protect. And your jealous thoughts, emotions, and behavior are accompanied by shame and guilt. If you struggle with jealousy, you may have doubted your own sanity—even doubted your right to have any jealous feelings at all. Our culture sometimes gives us the message that painful and difficult emotions are not allowed and, if you have them, there is something terribly wrong with you. But I want you to know that jealousy can be part of being human, having intimacy, and engaging in intense relationships.

People often get advice from well-meaning friends, or even therapists, that won't help and may actually make things worse. Here are some of the things you may have heard, and also the reasons why they aren't accurate or helpful.

- **"You must have low self-esteem."** The reality is that jealousy can also be a result of high self-esteem. Perhaps you won't let people treat you unfairly. It's not this simple.

- **"You have to get your mind off this."** Trying not to think of jealousy will lead the jealous thoughts to bounce back. We must learn to accept the thoughts we have, without being ruled by them.

- **"Try to think positively."** This often makes people feel worse because, if this is the best advice that you can get, it will seem hopeless.

- **"Why are you punishing yourself?"** This misses the point entirely, because jealousy is an attempt to *protect* yourself from betrayal.

- **"You have no right to feel jealous."** Everyone has a right to whatever feelings and thoughts that he or she has. Invalidating you this way will only make you feel more threatened by rejection.

- **"I haven't done anything wrong."** That may be true, but when the person who is the focus of your jealousy says this, it might lead you to work harder at finding out what seems hidden.

- **"You should just trust me."** Being ordered to trust someone seldom works because it doesn't validate your struggle or the reasons why you feel the way you do.

- **"You are screwed up."** This only adds to fears of rejection and abandonment, which increase the likelihood of jealousy.

While any of these statements might be valid, none helps because they are not relevant to the way you feel and do not help you cope with those feelings. Because jealousy is based on a feeling that a relationship is threatened, offering criticism, dismissal, or ridicule will only make you feel worse about yourself—and even more jealous. So how can you get a handle on your jealousy in a way that actually helps?

Showing you how is one of my goals in this book. I want to help you understand what jealousy is, because it is a passionate emotion that includes many other emotions that trouble us, including anger, anxiety, helplessness, resentment, and hopelessness. I also want to help you realize that you are not alone in your feelings.

Another goal is to look at the choices you make, which can either sabotage your relationship or save it. Once you feel jealous—once you have the intense feeling that someone cannot be trusted—what do you do next? Jealous thoughts and feelings lead to some common patterns of reaction and behavior, such as:

- Interrogating

- Looking for clues of betrayal

- Trying to control someone

- Inflicting punishments

- Worrying obsessively over a possible betrayal

- Dreading what you fear will happen if you are betrayed

But jealous thoughts and feelings don't always have to lead to jealous behavior. You can make a choice about what you actually do. And there are better ways to respond. This book teaches you what to do with the thoughts and feelings. Even if you can't get jealousy out of your mind completely, you can act in ways that keep it from taking over and wrecking your well-being and your relationships.

This book is not meant to lecture you on the idea that you have no right to your jealous feelings, or that you are irrational, or that you should "just get over it." No. When jealousy has justification, it may be time to get assertive, problem-solve with your partner, and set some limits. Jealous triggers may lead the two of you to become clearer about your commitment to each other, develop some guidelines, and establish mutual understanding— all pathways to building trust. Sometimes jealousy can tell us about what our relationship needs more of, whether it's commitment, honesty, transparency, or choice.

Your jealous feelings don't mean that something terrible is about to happen. It helps to look at reality—not just your thoughts and feelings. Emotions are not always accurate predictors of reality. Because jealousy is such a passionate and overwhelming emotion, standing back and getting some distance from it may seem impossible. But if you slow down your thinking, step aside from your feelings for a few moments, and reflect on what you are telling yourself, maybe things can change. Maybe you don't have to be hijacked by thoughts and feelings.

If you are the object of a partner's jealousy, this book can help you understand what your partner is going through. It can help you see why dismissive responses will never help. As the object of jealousy, you know how hard it is to feel accused and distrusted in the context of your intimate relationship. You can both learn better ways of coping with these painful feelings. This book will guide you and your partner to work together to find common understanding and guidelines. Jealousy will not go away simply because you want it to. In fact, it may be something that both of you can learn to accept, live with, and even respect—while decreasing the negative behaviors and arguments that result from it.

The ultimate goal of this book is to help you see that, because jealousy is not inherently bad and is part of human nature, it is not blameworthy or something to be ashamed about. It can actually be useful by helping you discover areas in your relationship that need attention. I've helped hundreds of clients understand their jealousy and find freedom from the misery it can bring. Read on and see how you can find freedom too.

Part I

About the Passion of Jealousy

Chapter 1

The Evolution of Competitive Emotions

Even the most rational and logical person can feel overwhelmed by jealousy and hijacked by the anger, anxiety, and helplessness that it entails. Evolutionary psychologist David Buss recalls that when he was in college, he believed that if a girlfriend wished to have sex with other people, then he had no right to protest—he didn't own her body. She should feel free to do whatever she wished to do. But when he got a girlfriend, he changed his mind.[1] He is not alone. Almost everyone feels the same way.

Of all the emotions we can experience, jealousy is perhaps the most difficult one to deal with—and the most dangerous. Jealousy is passion directed against the threat of betrayal or the threat of abandonment. It's anger at someone we view as an intruder or a competitor. It's resentment at the person who we fear might abuse our trust. It is visceral, fundamental, and sometimes violent. We can feel overwhelmed, carried away, and controlled by jealousy. Our heart and mind get hijacked. And we feel lost in anxiety and helplessness.

What Is Jealousy?

Jealousy occurs when we fear that our *special relationship* is threatened. We fear that our partner or friend will lose interest in us and form a closer relationship with someone else. We feel threatened by their attention to this person. Jealousy does not occur in a vacuum—it is actually about *three people*. It is the third person who threatens our special relationship. We can be jealous of our lover, friends, family members, and coworkers. We can, if we are unfortunate, perceive threats from almost anyone who enters our social sphere. We fear that things may unravel rapidly and that we will be humiliated, marginalized, and abandoned.

We often confuse jealousy with envy. Envy occurs when we believe that someone has achieved an *advantage* over us—sometimes unfairly—and we resent their success because we think it reflects poorly on us. Their *success* is our *failure*. We are envious of people who compete in an area that we value: If it's business, we envy someone who is making more money or who gets promoted instead of us. If it's academics, we envy someone who gets a grant or publishes an article.

Envy is about *comparison*. Jealousy is about the *threat to a relationship*. Although jealousy and envy are different emotions, we often feel both of them about the same person because both are about our sense that we are in competition with others—and that we might lose.[2] I will be focusing on jealousy in this book.

How We Experience Jealousy

Jealousy is not a single emotion—it's a mix of many powerful, confusing feelings, such as anger, anxiety, dread, confusion, excitement, helplessness, hopelessness, and sadness. In fact, someone in a romantic relationship can feel jealous about perceived infidelity while also feeling sexually aroused about the fantasy of that infidelity. We get so confused because we tend to believe that we should have only one feeling at a time. Plus, there's love in the mix. The painful negative feelings can blend with our positive feelings of love. We want to feel just one way—either positive or negative—but we have both kinds of feelings, often coming in waves, often overwhelming us.

We say that we "feel" jealous, but our jealousy also involves a wide range of types of *thoughts*. We think, "He is interested in someone else" or "She will leave me" or "My partner should never find anyone else attractive." We have thoughts about what we should know: "I need to know exactly what is going on." And, if we don't know what's going on, we have thoughts about that: "What I don't know will hurt me."

We often take *action* on our jealousy by seeking reassurance and asking pointed questions. We might follow her, spy on him, read her email and text messages, seduce him, cajole her, check his GPS in the car, smell her perfume, go through his suitcase, ask other people what they know, and threaten our partner. We yell, interrogate, pout, withdraw. We cling or we avoid.

So jealousy is not "just a feeling." It is a host of emotions, sensations, thoughts, behaviors, questions, and strategies to control the other person. Jealousy is driven by the insatiable desire to *know for sure what is going on*, which leads us to imagine all the terrible things that we do not know, but that could be true. We seek to know and control. And we often treat our thoughts, fantasies, and feelings as if they are the very reality that we fear. But feelings are not facts.

Simply having a jealous feeling or thought is not the main problem. The problems come with all the behaviors and control strategies that follow. It's the *response* that gets us in trouble. A chain reaction of anxiety can unravel so quickly that we are completely surprised by what we are saying and doing. In other words, it's one thing to feel jealous and it's another thing to act on it. We will explore this in more detail later. First, for you to get more control over jealous reactions, it's helpful to understand jealousy better, both your own and jealousy in general. Here's the big picture.

Looking to Evolution

Darwin's great insight helped us realize that the history of all species is the struggle for survival.[3] Our ancestors were threatened by starvation, attacks by strangers, murder by members of their own tribe or community, rape, and infanticide. Life was a struggle from birth. And the struggle was often against each other. We can think of many qualities that seem essential to human nature—attachment in infants, defense against threats, fear of heights, an infant's fear of strangers, public speaking anxiety, forming strong attachments to a partner and our children—and recognize that each of them is found in many other species because each contributes to survival.

Survival is about winning against the competition. There is competition between siblings, colleagues, and sexual suitors. Jealousy is a primordial recognition of these threats. It is a strategy that evolved to protect us. But in our world today, it may destroy a marriage, drive away friends, and alienate brothers and sisters.

Does this mean jealousy is justified and that there is nothing we can do to control it? Absolutely not. Knowing that jealousy has roots in our evolution does not justify jealous rage, suspicion, or retaliation. We can be driven by fears and anxieties that were useful 100,000 years ago, but are now dysfunctional. What worked in the past may fail us today.

Understanding the evolutionary model can help us understand why the passion of jealousy is so powerful, so intensely emotional. But like our fears of heights, water, dogs, being in closed spaces, or walking in an open field, the fears that fuel jealousy have outlived their usefulness. The environment relevant to the evolutionary perspective is not our cities, suburbs, and towns in the twenty-first century. Evolution does not justify jealousy. It only helps us understand why it is so universal and powerful. We didn't choose to have the brain that evolved with these fears.

In the long-gone days of our ancient ancestors, who were continually threatened, *life was about survival,* with survival of genes being most important. A person may have died in a fight, but if his genes survived, then he passed the evolutionary fitness test, as his traits continued into the next generation. Two things are essential for evolutionary fitness: procreation and the survival of offspring. Someone can procreate and have many babies, but if they all die, then fitness dies with them. If no one takes care of the babies, then the genes will not survive. This is where jealousy comes in.

The Evolution of Jealousy

Evolution helps us understand the passion and zeal behind jealousy: the blind rage that hijacks us so quickly that we are later astounded at our own feelings and actions; the terrifying fear that our partner will mate with someone else; the ways we can detect deception; the ability to deceive others. We are driven by instinctive passions that protected our ancestors for hundreds of thousands of years—but these protections can defeat our current interests. There are two relevant evolutionary theories: *parental investment theory* and *competition for limited resources.* Let's take a look at them.

Parental Investment Theory

This theory proposes that we are going to be more committed, in sharing resources and taking care of the young, if we have a high genetic investment in the other person's survival.[4] We are more likely to protect and support individuals who share genes, such as our biological children, siblings, and close relatives. We are less likely to protect and support biologically unrelated individuals.

In this way, jealousy is a *protective strategy.* If a man is uncertain of the paternity of his partner's offspring, he may end up taking care of a stranger's genes—thereby sacrificing the possibility of passing on his genes. Because a woman always knows that infants carry her genes, her jealousy is less determined by paternity or sexual behavior, and more influenced by her concern for the protection and resources that a male partner contributes. A woman will want to ensure that she receives protection and support from her male partner because this increases the survival of offspring. Both will defend against competitors. Males and females become jealous when their genetic investment is threatened.

Consistent with this theory, research shows that men are more likely to feel jealous over perceived *sexual infidelity* because it calls paternity into question. Women are more likely to experience jealousy when they perceive *emotional closeness* between a partner and another woman, because this suggests that resources and protection will be provided to someone else. While men and women can have both kinds of jealous feelings, men are more likely to express *sexual jealousy* while women are more likely to express *attachment jealousy*.[5]

If jealousy has an evolutionary basis, we should find it in other cultures. And we do. In fact, the gender difference—males being more concerned with sexual infidelity and females with emotional infidelity—has been found in the United States, Germany, the Netherlands, and China.[6] At the same time, these evolutionary predispositions are affected by cultural differences. In cultures where honor is emphasized, jealousy is much stronger in males. We are all too familiar with "honor killings" in countries like Pakistan or Bangladesh. And the dishonor of infidelity can cause a woman who was raped to marry the rapist or be stoned to death.

Competition for Limited Resources

The second evolutionary theory of jealousy stresses competition for resources. This helps us understand jealousy in infants and jealousy between siblings. Because siblings can be in competition with each other for food and protection from their parents, jealousy can arise—and often does. Infants can be jealous of attention that their mother directs toward another baby. In a study of six-month-old infants, researchers found that babies show signs of distress and attempt to attract the mother's attention more when the mother interacts with another baby than when she plays with a nonhuman object.[7] A real baby is more of a threat than an inanimate object.

> Four-year-old Gary was both excited and apprehensive about his new sister, Phyllis. But as she grew, he felt there was a threat to his special relationship with Mom and Dad. He alternated between playing with Phyllis and grabbing things from her, and even began to regress to more babyish behavior.

Why would siblings be in competition with one another? Food resources were scarce during most of the evolution of our species. Siblings had to compete for food, attention, and protection. Some species overproduce offspring and, as a result, offspring can die from starvation. This overproduction of offspring might be viewed as a strategy to ensure that some of them survive. But it leads to competition among siblings, sometimes to the death. Pigs often produce more offspring in a litter than the number of teats available to feed them. Piglets that are not strong and competitive will die. Evolutionary theorists describe this tendency to overproduce offspring as "warehousing." As grim as this may sound, it points to the fundamental nature of jealousy in a *competitive world.*

Sibling rivalry makes sense. Similarly, in a world of scarcity, being excluded from friendships and alliances could also be detrimental. If my prehistoric ancestors were marginalized by their peers in the tribe, then they were less likely to enjoy the benefits of a hunt. And they would have died from starvation. Which means that I wouldn't be here.

Jealousy is common across species. When owners of pets described what they perceived as jealousy in their pets, the following rank was observed: dogs (81 percent), horses (79 percent), cats (66 percent), birds (67 percent), and rats (47 percent).[8] Dogs express jealousy toward other dogs, and will growl, stalk, and place themselves between their human master and other dogs. I know that our two male cats—Danny and Frankie—started with a wonderful relationship when we got Frankie at four weeks of age. They played and slept together; they groomed each other. However, as Frankie grew to adulthood and became a large, alpha cat, he was quite jealous of any attention given to Danny, which was made clear through his aggressive behavior. Just as we humans are jealous, so are our pets. We share the two common evolutionary issues behind jealousy.

A Historical Perspective

Stories of jealousy are older than the written word. Cain's jealousy of Abel taints humanity's beginnings in Genesis. It also marks the nature of the Judeo-Christian God's relationship with his people, enshrined in the First Commandment and proclaimed in the book of Exodus, "Thou shalt not bow down thyself to them, nor serve them: for I the LORD thy God am a jealous God."[9]

Jealousy was central to Greek mythology and literature. The goddess Hera was jealous about the many other women who attracted the attention of her husband, Zeus. When Jason betrayed his wife, Medea, she murdered their children in revenge. Helen's betrayal of her husband, Menelaus, sparked the Trojan War.

In medieval Europe, jealousy was viewed as a necessary, even positive, emotion that was linked to honor. The twelfth-century author Andreas Capellanus described the importance of intensity in love and jealousy in his book *The Art of Courtly Love*. He wrote: "Love cannot exist in the individual who cannot be jealous" and "Suspicion of the beloved generates jealousy and therefore intensifies love."[10] For the noble knight pursuing love, it was dishonorable not to fight when "provoked" to jealousy. In Shakespeare's *Othello*, the malicious Iago tricks Othello into becoming jealous by casting doubt on the fidelity of his wife, Desdemona. Othello describes his jealousy—which leads him to murder his faithful wife—as the emotion "of one that loved not wisely, but too well."[11] While his actions were horrific, they were done out of love and honor. He is therefore the tragic hero of the play—not the villain.

In the nineteenth century, jealousy came to be increasingly viewed as interfering with domestic harmony. The Victorian period emphasized domestic tranquility and controlling powerful emotions. Jealousy was effectively banned, because it was considered disruptive to the harmony of the Victorian family.

Today, in America and throughout much of Western Europe, jealousy is something we are expected to be ashamed of and to hide. Surveys indicate that Americans are more likely than people in other Western cultures to believe that their jealousy is a sign that there is something wrong with them.[12] In a sense, *jealousy went underground*. No longer a badge of love and honor, it has become a symbol of inability to trust, lack of self-control, neurosis, and shame. But it definitely has not gone away, neither in popular culture nor in our lives. Popular songs—like "I Heard It Through the Grapevine," "Every Breath You Take," "Hey Jealousy," and "Jealous Guy"—show that we are never alone with this emotion. And today there are more venues for infidelity, contacting strangers, downloading pornography, or having a secret rendezvous online. Each of these "opportunities" can make some of us more insecure, creating an overwhelming sense of uncertainty. In the new millennium, we're surrounded by insecurity-provoking media, from relentless messages about what our bodies should look like to totally unrealistic depictions of sex in pornography. It's easier to "spy" on each other, but not easier to know the truth about each other. If we want to feed our jealousy, there's plenty of fuel out there.

Jealousy in Stepfamilies

While we tend to think that jealousy happens most often in intimate relationships, it can also be a problem in any important relationships. Jealousy is often an issue in "reconstituted families," in which children contend with divorced parents, stepparents, stepbrothers, and stepsisters. There are 100 million Americans in a stepfamily relationship and 35 percent of all married-couple households include stepchildren.[13] There is even a website in the UK for stepparents who feel competitive with, or who resent, their stepchildren.[14] When parents divorce and there is a new partner for Mom or Dad, children have feelings of betrayal, anger, anxiety, resentment—in a word, *jealousy*.

> Kara was in her thirties and married when she learned that her divorced dad had a new partner he wanted her to meet. Like many adult children of divorced parents, this new part of the family dynamic triggered resentment: "How can he think I would want to meet her? He just dumped Mom. He lied to me about their marriage. How can I trust him?" She viewed her dad's new partner as an unwelcome interloper—a poacher—who had torn the family apart. Kara felt that her special relationship with her father was over, that his new partner would replace her and her brother, and that she had to be loyal to her mother. All of this meant she had to hold on to her resentment for her dad.

Jealousy at Work

Job security is continually in question, as it's a rather rare thing to have. In 2012, the average tenure of a job was 4.2 years.[15] As a consequence, there is a wide range of opportunities for jealousy: "Jake gets the better assignments." "Donna was promoted—I should be too!" "Eric always goes out to lunch with our boss, and I'm never invited." "Everyone seems to win the excellent-service award but me." Status in a company dynamic can depend on whom the boss favors—and who gets included or excluded.

> Marianne often felt that her colleagues excluded her: "They don't ask me out. They do things without me." She withdrew, even while complaining that the boss was not promoting her. This resentment and jealousy became a wedge between her and everyone else at work. Feeling excluded, she began to exclude herself. And things spiraled down.

Jealousy Gets Boosted by Social Media

Social media gives all of us opportunities to feel that we have been snubbed, rejected, or left to fend for ourselves because others seem to enjoy the friendships and relationships that we have always wanted for ourselves. We say to ourselves: "Why wasn't I invited to that party?" "Is there a reason I wasn't tagged?" "Her life is perfect, there's so much missing from mine." "If only I could afford to travel like he does."

> When Paul looked at Ron's Facebook posts, he noticed that Ron was with Larry, Ken, and Nancy on a boat trip, enjoying themselves—without Paul. He burned with resentment and felt publicly humiliated, as he was reminded that he was left out once again.

Take-Home Messages

There are a number of important points in this chapter that can help you understand that you are not alone. I offer this summary to bring the messages home.

- Jealousy is a powerful emotion that includes anxiety, anger, helplessness, hopelessness, and sadness

- There is a difference between "feeling" jealous and "acting" on the jealousy

- You are not alone—almost anyone can be provoked to feel jealous

- Evolution built jealousy into human nature

- Jealousy is a protective strategy that is based on parental investment (protecting genetic investment in offspring) and competition for resources (sibling rivalry)

- Male jealousy is more focused on sexual threats while female jealousy is more focused on emotional closeness

- Jealousy has a long history, from ancient times to the present

- Jealousy can be found in infants, children, animals, and many cultures

You can now recognize that jealousy is part of human nature and that its power and passion may come from instinctive responses that hijack us. This is an important foundation for you to have as you consider your own struggles with jealousy. In the next chapter, you can evaluate your own jealousy and examine how it impacts your relationships. And in the following chapters, you can look at how jealousy is related to your history of relationships, your personality, and your beliefs. The more you understand jealousy and your experience of it, the better you will be able to cope with these feelings.

Chapter 2

Is Jealousy a Problem for You?

All of us are vulnerable to feeling jealous at times, so the question to consider is: Has jealousy become a problem for you? You have a right to your feelings, but it's important to take a look at how much jealousy is affecting your daily life. You can assess whether jealousy is getting in the way of your intimate relationship, friendships, family relationships, and interactions with coworkers. Do you...

- Complain, pout, ruminate, resent, avoid, or disparage family, friends, and colleagues because of your jealous feelings?

- Has jealousy led to relationships ending abruptly?

- Do you hold on to resentments for long periods of time?

- Have you complained to colleagues, and does doing this ever put your job at risk?

- Do you find that you can't step away from your jealous thoughts and feelings?

- Do they hijack you so that you feel you have no choices in your actions?

- Does your jealousy make you depressed?

- Do you sometimes feel hopeless, not only about your current relationship but also about your ability to have a relationship without being overwhelmed by jealousy?

- Has your jealousy led you to say things that you later regret saying?

You can make an honest assessment of your jealous thoughts, feelings, and behaviors by filling out a questionnaire. The questionnaire assesses answers to thirty questions, which are related to triggers for jealousy and how you respond to them.

The Jealousy Scale

This scale assesses a range of possible responses and the frequency of your jealous feelings. The focus is on how you are experiencing, and responding to, events in your relationship. Your answers do not mean that you have no right to your feelings, thoughts, or behaviors. And they do not mean that your partner is completely innocent or that you have nothing to be jealous about. This scale is written to address jealousy for intimate partners and heterosexual couples, so if you are part of a gay couple you can think about your partner or spouse. If you are not currently in a relationship, think back about past relationships.

Try to answer each question as accurately as possible. Don't try to be rational, reasonable, or well adjusted. Think about each question in terms of how you would answer it when you get upset or bothered. There are no right or wrong answers. We are interested in how you think, feel, act, and communicate when certain things happen in your relationship.

Rate the following behaviors, thoughts, and feelings that you have engaged in because of your jealous thoughts and feelings.

On a piece of paper, write down the number that indicates how often you engage them.

Never   0

Rarely   1

Sometimes   2

Often   3

Always   4

1. I question my partner about his or her past relationships.

2. I get upset when I hear about his or her past relationships.

3. I compare myself with his or her past partners and this bothers me.

4. I question my partner to find out what is going on.

5. I ask my partner whom he or she was talking to, or sitting near, when out without me.

6. I try to interrupt conversations my partner has with others of the opposite sex.

7. I try to check my partner's emails or texts.

8. I check my partner's phone calls or messages.

9. I check my partner's GPS to find out where he or she has been.

10. I seek out reassurance from my partner that I can trust him or her.

11. I withdraw from my partner when I am suspicious.

12. I accuse my partner of being interested in someone else.

13. I plead with my partner not to flirt with others.

14. I criticize my partner or say negative things about people I think he or she might be interested in.

15. I try to make my partner feel guilty.

16. I try to provoke my partner to get into an argument when I am jealous.

17. I try to seduce my partner to get reassurance or to feel better when I am jealous.

18. I follow my partner to find out what is going on.

19. I threaten my partner with a breakup, separation, or divorce.

20. I threaten my partner with violence.

21. I have been violent when I have been jealous.

22. I try to keep my partner from leaving or doing things.

23. I criticize myself to my partner.

24. I look for alternative partners.

25. I flirt with other people to try to make my partner jealous.

26. I don't trust my partner.

27. I worry that my partner might be unfaithful.

28. I don't like it when my partner has colleagues or friends of the opposite sex who might be attractive to him or her.

29. I get upset if my partner touches or kisses someone, or dances with someone else.

30. I get upset if someone of the opposite sex seems interested in my partner.

Look at your responses to the questions. Does a pattern emerge? Do you get anxious, angry, or upset when you think about your partner and other people? If you answered "Sometimes" to four or more of these questions, then jealousy may be a problem in your current or past relationships. If your total score exceeds 12, you are probably experiencing significant distress at times due to jealousy.

Coping with Jealous Feelings

The next thing to look at is how you cope with your jealous feelings—what do you actually do? This includes interrogating, checking, following, withdrawing, and other behaviors.

- Are you talking to your partner as if he or she needs to defend himself or herself?

- Are you insinuating that he or she cannot be trusted?

- Are you checking his or her social media, phone, email, GPS?

- Are you asking other people what they know?

- Are you pouting, withdrawing, making yourself unavailable, withholding sex?

You may attempt to limit or control your partner's actions—trying to prevent him or her from meeting people you are threatened by.

- Do you try to convince your partner not to socialize with certain people because of your jealousy?

- Do you tell your partner that you need to accompany him or her when socializing?

- Do you tell your partner that he or she must check in with you frequently when not around you?

- Do you ask other people to report on your partner?

Jealousy may lead you to dwell on the past, or what is going on currently, in your mind. It can lead you to worry about the future—what your partner might do or how you would cope without him or her. Consider how jealousy leads you to think about experiences with colleagues, friends, and family members.

- Do you ruminate about your partner's past relationships?

- Do you frequently compare yourself to his or her past partners?

- Do you feel worse about your current relationship or yourself when you think about your partner's past relationships?

- Do you think that your partner will seek out other people and betray you?

Jealousy can also be related to your doubts about yourself.

- Do you think that, if other people are interesting and attractive to your partner, this means you are inferior?

- Do you conclude that, if a friend is spending more time with someone else, you are boring?

Jealousy can affect your relationship in many ways. Consider whether any of these statements apply to your experience with a partner, family member, friend, or coworker.

- Having more arguments

- Withdrawing

- Clinging

- Demanding

- Fighting

- Avoiding

- Feeling miserable in the relationship

- Having sex less often

- Feeling less affection

As you look at the ways you cope with jealousy, consider Ken's experience. Ken has been dating Louise for seven months. She was active sexually before she met Ken, and Ken also had a number of girlfriends and sexual experiences. But Ken now worries that he might not be able to trust Louise. As he responded to the Jealousy Scale and considered the questions about coping, he saw that:

- He believes Juan, whom Louise describes as a friend, is interested in a romantic or sexual relationship with her

- He thinks she might be interested in Juan as more than a friend

- He is very displeased that she occasionally works with other young men on projects at work

- He questions Louise about her text messages with Juan and other men

- He checks her Facebook page to see whether there are any pictures of her with any men, especially Juan

- He questions her about what she did the previous night

- He accuses her of being interested in Juan

- He has tried to hack into her email account

- He has considered following her

Although nothing has turned up to indicate that Louise is unfaithful, he "needs to find out for sure" that she can be trusted.

Imagining Life Without Jealousy

You may not be as jealous as Ken is—or you may be more jealous. Either way, answering these questions should give you a sense of whether or not jealousy is beginning to take over your life. Now that you have gone through the questions, think about how you would feel if you were feeling less jealous.

- How would your relationship improve?

- Would you be able to communicate better if you were less overwhelmed by your jealousy?

- Would you feel less anxious, less sad, or less regretful of things that you say or do?

- How would your partner think of you if you were less jealous?

This is not to say that you don't have a right to your feelings. The purpose of this chapter is to help you perceive the degree to which these feelings overwhelm you, preoccupy you, and interfere with a range of experiences inside and outside your relationship. In the next chapter, we will look at how your history of relationships and your beliefs about relationships can contribute to jealousy.

Chapter 3

Attachment and Commitment

When Steve was a kid, his parents always seemed to be fighting. When Dad would come home, Mom seemed angry, agitated, and worried. "Where have you been?" she would yell. A couple of times, Dad had moved out—once for a week, another time for two months—but he always came back. Steve worried that Dad would never come back. And he worried, too, that if Mom left, then Steve would be alone, without anyone to take care of him. He would sit in his room, crying and thinking, "They're going to leave me alone." He would often fake being sick so that he could stay home from school to be with Mom. It was where he felt safe. He couldn't stand the idea of sleep-away camp. When Steve was eleven, he learned that Dad had been having affairs. Mom would yell at Dad, saying he was a bum and that she couldn't trust him.

Like Steve, your history of close relationships may still be affecting you. Experiences from childhood and throughout your life can set the stage for distrust, worries about betrayal, and the feeling that you can't rely on people. If your parents threatened separation, if there was sickness in the family—or death—you may have developed the belief that people you rely on will leave. Your jealousy fears today may reflect emotional injuries from the past.

Your Attachment Style

We differ from one another in how secure we feel in our attachment to others. Our attachment style begins to emerge during infancy. Infants tend to show one of four different types of behavior when their mothers or fathers leave the room.

- Some infants are more anxious than others. A baby may cry, protest, bang its hands, and may seem desperately afraid.

- Babies may have an "anxious-ambivalent" style of attachment, protesting when Mom leaves the room, but showing anger or aloofness when she returns.

- Some have an "avoidant" style, in which they seem to remain somewhat attached, but they often appear wary of getting close to Mom.

- Others have a secure attachment. They can tolerate Mom leaving the room, and show enthusiasm when she returns. Securely attached infants are comfortable when alone and they are more likely to explore their environment, knowing that they have a secure base because they trust that Mom will return.

According to *attachment theory*, infants have an innately predisposed tendency to maintain closeness to the main parental figure—usually, but not always, the mother.[16] An infant's attachment is based on the adaptive value of the relationship with a caretaker—for protection, support, food, and the opportunity to socialize.

When an infant begins to recognize that a mother's return is predictable—that he or she can rely on Mom coming back—the infant builds up a belief that she is reliable, trustworthy, responsive, and caring. This provides a sense of security for the infant. It allows him or her to explore the environment away from the mother and to self-soothe in her absence. Alternatively, an infant may develop expectations that a caretaker cannot be relied on, does not care, or is not responsive.[17] Attachment theorists believe that these styles continue throughout life and affect how we relate in a variety of close relationships—especially intimate relationships.

If your expectation of a committed relationship is that the other person is not responsive, not reliable, threatens separation, and cannot be trusted, then your adult relationships may be at risk.

Your Early Attachments

Look back on your attachments and relationships in childhood. Consider these common scenarios and see whether any apply to you.

- **Did you worry that one or both parents might leave you, or that they might get sick or die?** This may lead you to fear sudden loss or abandonment as an adult.

- **Were there threats of separation or divorce, or an actual separation or divorce?** This may have resulted in a fear that your closest relationship could fall apart.

- **Did your family move a lot?** If you attended different schools or lived in different neighborhoods, relationships with other kids may have been cut short. Maybe they picked on you or weren't loyal. This could lead to fears that being on your own will leave you in an unfriendly world where people will not be supportive, where you will be isolated.

- **Did someone you dated let you down, even cheated on you?** Your dating history may have resulted in a fear that someone will cheat on you, manipulate you, or suddenly leave you, so you may have become hyperfocused on these potential threats.

Your Experience in Close Relationships

It's helpful to look at your style of experience in close relationships because it can offer more insight into how you feel when intimacy begins to develop. Using this measure, you can evaluate how you feel in close relationships. Are you comfortable with closeness? Do you find closeness to be unpleasant, almost as if it is smothering or unnatural at times? Are you dependent—and needy? Are you anxious in your close relationships? Go through this Adult Attachment Scale for Close Relationships[18] and think about how you respond.

The following questions evaluate how you *generally* feel, so think about your past and present relationships with people who have been especially important to you, such as family members, romantic partners, and close friends. On a piece of paper, respond to each statement with a number between 1 and 5 that corresponds to this scale. Answering with a 1 indicates that the statement is not at all characteristic of you, a 5 indicates that it is very characteristic of you, and the other numbers indicate degrees in between.

Adult Attachment Scale for Close Relationships

1	2	3	4	5

Not at all characteristic of me   Very characteristic of me

1. I find it relatively easy to get close to people.

2. I find it difficult to allow myself to depend on others.

3. I often worry that other people don't really love me.

4. I find that others are reluctant to get as close as I would like.

5. I am comfortable depending on others.

6. I *don't* worry about people getting too close to me.

7. I find that people are never there when you need them.

8. I am somewhat *un*comfortable being close to others.

9. I often worry that other people won't want to stay with me.

10. When I show my feelings for others, I'm afraid they will not feel the same about me.

11. I often wonder whether other people really care about me.

12. I am comfortable developing close relationships with others.

13. I am *un*comfortable when anyone gets too emotionally close to me.

14. I know that people will be there when I need them.

15. I want to get close to people, but I worry about being hurt.

16. I find it difficult to trust others completely.

17. People often want me to be emotionally closer than I feel comfortable being.

18. I am not sure that I can always depend on people to be there when I need them.

Your responses to these statements fall into three categories: closeness, dependability, and anxiety. By scoring your answers to the statements relating to each one of these categories, you can get more clarity around your style. Items with an asterisk need to be reverse-scored, which means that even though you may have written down a 1 to rate your experience, you would score it with a 5. If you rated something a 2, score it as a 4. And vice versa. Neutral scores remain a 3. Add up the scores in each category.

The Closeness Scale: This measures the extent to which you are comfortable with closeness and intimacy. This relates to your responses to statements 1, 6, 8*, 12, 13*, and 17*. A high score here indicates that you are comfortable with closeness and intimacy, and a low score shows that you have difficulty getting close or allowing others to get close to you.

The Dependability Scale: This measures the extent to which you feel you can depend on others to be available when needed. Your responses to statements 2*, 5, 7*, 14, 16*, and 18* are part of this scale. A high score here indicates that you feel you can rely on and trust others, and a low score shows that it is difficult for you to depend on others.

The Anxiety Scale: This measures the extent to which you worry about being rejected or unloved, and is related to statements 3, 4, 9, 10, 11, and 15. A high score here indicates that you are anxious about people in close relationships, and a low score shows that you are not particularly anxious in these relationships.

When you consider what your responses to the statements in the scale indicate about your style, you may gain more clarity by asking yourself these questions.

- Do you find yourself comfortable, or uncomfortable, with closeness in relationships?

- If you are uncomfortable in a close relationship, what about closeness might bother you?

- In a close relationship, are you concerned that you might lose yourself, your identity might be threatened, or it may limit your freedom?

- Are you concerned about being controlled by someone?

- Do you feel that you can count on people, or do you think that they will disappoint you, hurt you, or not be helpful?

- Can you think of specific examples when others let you down?

- Are there examples of people you can count on?

- Do you often feel anxious in close relationships, as if people will leave you or that they don't care for you as much as you want or need?

- What are some examples of people leaving or not caring enough?

- Are there examples of relationships in which you don't feel anxious?

Like attachment styles, your comfort level with closeness is related to how jealous you feel. If you don't feel comfortable with closeness, you are *less likely* to be jealous. This is because you may not rely on the relationship as much for your happiness. But your avoidance of closeness may also make it difficult to develop an intimate relationship.[19] Someone is less likely to be jealous if they maintain some distance or are not close to their partner. Those with a secure attachment style are the least jealous.[20]

People who are insecure about their attachments are *more likely* to be jealous. If you are prone to anxiety in close relationships, you may be reluctant to get close because you fear losing the relationship. And, when you are close, your insecurity increases because you have more to lose and you fear you cannot cope with the loss.

Everyone differs in the desire for closeness, with some people feeling anxious about any threat to the relationship, and others feeling threatened by too much closeness. For example, the person who is the object of jealousy may feel that he or she is being controlled, engulfed, or overwhelmed by the demands of the jealous partner. He or she may therefore seek distance by putting up barriers to closeness that may feed into the jealousy narrative.

In close relationships, we often assume that we both want the same thing—but one person may want closeness while the other might prefer a parallel partner who is around, but never quite close to them. How does your partner feel about closeness?

Your Relationship History

You can also look at jealousy from the perspective of your personal history with relationships from childhood until the present moment.

> Brian learned that his father—who had portrayed himself as a pious churchgoer—had a series of relationships with women other than his mother. But Brian's brother didn't tell him until he was twenty years old, establishing for Brian the idea that people will hide the truth from him. This early sense of distrust contributed to his distrust of his wife.

If your childhood has included infidelity by one, or both, of your parents, you may trust people less. This may set a bias in your mind and you may think, "People can't be trusted in intimate relationships."

If your parents were not responsive to your needs, or not reliably meeting your needs, you may be prone to believing that you cannot trust your current partner to be there for you. If your parents invalidated your feelings and perceptions in ways that taught you that you cannot rely on what you think and feel, you may be prone to jealousy.

> Penny didn't trust her partner. When she was a kid, her mother would get angry with Penny if she needed something while her mother was on the phone with friends. Her mother never had time for her needs. As a result, Penny thought that her partner also couldn't be trusted because she believed that he would favor other people over her.

Your ability to trust people may also be affected by a history of problematic relationships. If you have chosen partners who are narcissistic and dishonest, you are more likely to believe that people cannot be trusted in relationships.

> Zoey was attracted to cool, unavailable men. She had a series of relationships with men who seemed exceptionally unable to make any commitments to her. At first, this sparked her interest because she conflated the fact that they were unattainable with the idea that they were desirable. And Zoey believed she'd be able to convince each of them that she was the right one for him. This inevitably led to heartbreak. She had several underlying beliefs: that she doesn't deserve a real commitment, that men who are unattainable are more interesting, and that the kind of guys who want commitment are usually boring. Zoey's attraction led to experiences that confirmed that men would betray her, she didn't deserve a

loyal partner, and she was doomed to one rejection or betrayal after another. Choosing someone who was honest, reliable, and—perhaps—a bit more boring would help her recognize that relationships don't have to be doomed.

In many cases, we could never predict that betrayal would happen. But it happened, and the effects stay with us.

Helen described her relationship with her husband as conventional—with three kids and a house in the suburbs, they celebrated holidays and attended church together. She thought she had the typical middle-class marriage, one that she could count on. But then, much to Helen's surprise, she learned that her husband had been carrying on an affair for a long time. After the divorce, she learned that he had had several affairs during their marriage. This set the stage for future distrust.

Your Commitment and Investment

Jealousy may depend on your level of commitment and your investment in a relationship. During the earliest stages of a relationship, there is little investment—so jealousy is minimal. If you only had one date with someone, you don't have much to lose. But as you get more involved, you have more invested, and you have more to lose.

When Steve began dating Rachel, he was attracted by a lot of things: she was beautiful to him, she had a great sense of humor, and she had a free spirit. Even though she came from a traditional background, she had experimented sexually and had lived on her own. He was excited getting to know her during the first few weeks of the relationship because he found her free spirit and experimentation with sex to be turn-ons. She was spontaneous, open, emotionally intense, and really interested in him. He felt little jealousy—Steve was just excited to be with Rachel. But after a few months passed and he fell in love with her, he became obsessed with jealous thoughts and feelings. He dwelled on her past experimentation and wondered if he was simply another experiment. The more committed he became, the more distrustful he felt.

Why did Steve suddenly become jealous? Because he had more to lose, but at the same time, he and Rachel were not in a settled commitment. During this middle part of the relationship, there is investment—but there is also *uncertainty*. You just don't know whether the relationship will last. It could end. This uncertainty makes jealousy more common during the middle phase before you make a commitment to being together.

As most relationships continue for years, jealousy decreases—unless, of course, someone has an affair. In a well-established, long-lasting relationship, there is less uncertainty so there is also less jealousy.[21] In a study of 100 college women, those in steady dating relationships were less likely to report jealousy than women not in steady relationships.[22]

Steve's jealousy had a lot to do with developing greater commitment and greater investment. Because increased commitment during this middle phase is associated with a greater likelihood of jealousy, it is important to look at how you view your partner's commitment. Some people are more likely to accept a promise of fidelity: "I won't see other people" or "I won't sleep with other people." This can be sufficient commitment for them, enough to trust. Others have their own criteria for how commitment is expressed. For example, if a partner spends a lot of time with friends or alone, some might view him or her as lacking commitment. Or they may think, "He only wants to see me a couple of times a week. That's not much of a commitment."

We each see the development of commitment differently: some of us are patient and can allow commitment to evolve as the relationship moves forward in time; some of us view commitment in all-or-nothing terms. Consider these common beliefs to gain insight into your style.

- My partner should spend almost all his or her leisure time with me

- My partner should contact me daily

- My partner should tell me that he or she loves me

- My partner should do things to make me feel special

- My partner should plan future activities with me

- My partner shouldn't have any secrets

This variety of ideas we can hold conveys that the two people in a relationship may have different ideas about commitment—especially when the relationship is developing. One person might want more independence, or may not be completely sure how they feel about the relationship. The other person might feel totally committed and sure. These differences can trigger a struggle. Commitment is usually something that develops with time and, in the earlier stages of a relationship, often one person is more committed than the other. One person can set up tests to see whether the other person has the kind of commitment that he or she is looking for. Negotiating commitment differences can be important to avoid putting your partner to the test.

Lynn felt that Mark lacked commitment because he often wanted to spend time with his guy friends hanging out, drinking, and going to parties—usually without her. She was patient at first, but after a couple of months she began to think that he just wasn't interested in the kind of committed relationship that she wanted. When she confronted him, he finally did acknowledge that he didn't like being "tied down" and wanted freedom "to be himself." So she broke off the relationship.

Lynn and Mark had different interests in closeness and commitment, and wanted different things. Mark wanted a compartmentalized relationship, whereas Lynn was hoping to find someone who might be a potential husband. Rather than trying to force him to want what she wanted, she decided to look elsewhere.

In the early stage of a relationship, there is little invested and little that can be lost, so jealousy is less likely to occur. As you develop more commitment and spend more time together, there is more to lose if the relationship ends—so there is a greater likelihood of jealousy. But simply spending time together may not equate a commitment and, as we have seen, we often differ from each other in how we define commitment. Some of us are comfortable with our partners having freedom to spend time with other people, while some of us may want more signs of commitment to the relationship. If we believe that our partners are truly committed to our relationship, we are less likely to experience jealousy.

The two of you need to come to terms with how you define this commitment. The question is: Do the two of you want the same thing? Trying to coerce someone into complying with your wishes can set the stage for greater conflict.

Emotional Intimacy

Your jealousy will also depend on the emotional intimacy that you experience with your partner. The greater the intimacy, the more vulnerable you are to fearing the loss of that intimacy. We are seldom jealous in relationships that we view as shallow or casual. In fact, some people purposely wish to maintain superficial relationships so that they minimize the risk of being hurt by betrayal or rejection. If the relationship is perceived as superficial, then there is less to feel jealous about. But nothing ventured, nothing gained.

> Eloise said, "I just want to be that party girl, you know, the one who dances on the bar drunk without her bra. I don't want to fall for that nice guy who I could love, because I know he'll hurt me. I know I won't be able to count on him. This way, I know it won't work out so I know I won't really get hurt."

Avoiding intimacy is more common than one might expect. We often assume that everyone is looking for commitment and intimacy, but Eloise was rejected by her partner a few years before and it led her to try to commit suicide. As a result, she equated intimacy and trust with overwhelming devastation. By maintaining a shallow persona, it was easier for her to reject anyone who was really interested in a serious relationship as a "loser." If you are in a relationship with someone who avoids intimacy, and you want intimacy, jealousy can arise because you have conflicting expectations.

When intimacy issues are involved, some people may actually try to provoke a jealous response in their partners. Doing this is a way of seeking reassurance that a partner is committed because when he or she engages in jealous behaviors, you can feel reassured. However, the very nature of jealous expressions—interrogating, withdrawing, demanding reassurance, and threatening—can increase the uncertainty in the relationship. The object of the jealousy may back away, counterattack, or threaten to leave the relationship, thereby adding even more anxiety to fears of betrayal and abandonment. All the same, research shows that when we perceive that our partner is jealous, we believe that he or she will never leave. The result is that we test partners by trying to make them feel jealous.

Other reasons to intentionally make partners feel jealous include punishing them for something they have done and competing with them if they are flirting with someone else. In some cases, people even "hedge their bets" and flirt with other people to ensure they have an alternative should a current relationship end. They might flirt with other people to boost self-esteem and prove that they are still attractive.

If any of these motives for making a partner jealous ring true, you might ask yourself, "What kinds of things can I do to provoke jealousy?," and consider the conflict that results. Is this conflict with your partner worth it? It often takes two to have a jealousy problem. You are not going to build security by playing the jealousy game.

Uncertainty and Worry

Uncertainty is the main issue in jealousy—and in anxiety. If you are uncertain about the relationship, you are more likely to feel threatened that your partner might become interested in someone else. This is especially true when you have some investment in the relationship. New friendships or opportunities for your partner to interact with new people may increase this sense of uncertainty, and you may begin to worry.

Uncertainty is an important element in worry: worriers equate uncertainty with a bad outcome and they view uncertainty as unacceptable.[23] If you are prone to worry, you may believe that it will reduce or eliminate uncertainty, and that checking, collecting information, and seeking reassurance will eliminate uncertainty. You may think, "I don't know for sure that she is faithful, and I need to know so I can relax," "I can't accept not knowing for sure—I need to know," or "I need to know *right now*."

Uncertainty and the Need to Know

While you might view worry as a way to get certainty, when you don't find proof, you are left with the uncertainty that the evidence is still to be discovered. You think, "Maybe there is something I don't know" and "I need to find out now!" The combination of a tendency to worry and perceived, or actual, uncertainty of the relationship will add to your jealous preoccupations. Research supports this, as the greater the perceived uncertainty in the relationship, the greater the likelihood of jealousy.[24] Not knowing becomes believing that what you don't know will hurt you. But as you demand complete certainty, your attempts to gain sufficient information will inevitably fail. Because the problem with uncertainty is that you can never have *absolute uncertainty*. In fact, you can be married for ten years and still not know for sure that you can trust your partner.

> Brian had been married to Sharon for fourteen years, and his sense of uncertainty increased when she began taking more business trips. He said, "Because I don't know for sure what she's up to, it's possible that she might cheat on me. I just don't want to be caught by surprise. I think I can find out what is going on by following her when she is here and by checking her email. But it is driving me crazy. Then I begin questioning her, which really pisses her off, and she tells me that I am driving her crazy. She pulls away, which makes me feel worse."

Brian is like a lot of people who are caught up in jealousy—to him, uncertainty is an intolerable condition and it predicts betrayal. He wants to avoid surprise, but he lives every day in the miserable clutches of his jealousy. "How can I ever know for sure?" he asked, his voice cracking as he tried to keep from crying.

Uncertainty and Geographical Distance

It's true that geographical distance adds to uncertainty. Some people try to make relationships work even though they are separated by hundreds, or even thousands, of miles. And some do make it work. But the distance, which makes it difficult to see each other, can add to uncertainty. When I gather personal histories of relationships, many people tell me that they tried to continue with a high-school sweetheart despite attending colleges separated by hundreds of miles. Sometimes, it works. I have a friend who met his future wife when he was fourteen. She went to a college far from his, they married in their senior year, and they are still married today. So it can work. But not always. For most people, distance and uncertainty wear on them.

> Julie was trying to continue a relationship with a man after he moved away. They had been involved for eight years, but it was becoming increasingly more difficult to stay connected. They would see each other every three months, he made little effort to visit her, and she constantly wondered what he was up to.

Uncertainty and Forming Attachments to People Who Are Already Attached

You're likely to be filled with uncertainty when you form an attachment to someone involved with someone else.

> Katherine met a man at her high-school reunion and had a fling that weekend. He was married, had several children, and lived hundreds of miles away. She continued to see him, hoping that she could either convince him to leave his wife or that she could "compartmentalize" this relationship and just accept

seeing him when she could. She was sinking herself further into a no-win situation, as she struggled to balance anxiety and anger along with hopes of working things out.

The relationship was fraught with uncertainty. It may be best to keep things simple, with no triangulated relationships, no compartmentalizing, no settling for second best. You might think that you are sophisticated and can handle a situation like this, but my observation is that our human nature leads us to form attachments that we want to be exclusive. So fooling ourselves about accepting the arrangement is likely to backfire. In fact, the further you get into this kind of thing, the harder it may be to extricate yourself.

Part II

How Jealousy Becomes a Problem

Chapter 4

Hijacked by the Jealous Mind

Jealousy has a mind of its own. When we are jealous, we are often hijacked by thoughts and feelings that make us think that we are unraveling, that our world is falling apart, and that something needs to be done immediately. We think we need the answer right now, that our feelings will escalate unless we get rid of them immediately, and that our partner will betray us unless we control things right now. The alarms are going off, blaring, driving us mad. We are hijacked by the thoughts and feelings of the jealous mind.

All our emotions have evolved to tell us about our needs and any threats to our welfare. As described in chapter 1, jealousy is an evolved and complex emotion that has been maintained because it ties into our need to protect our genetic investment, and to ensure that offspring have the best protection and support that they can have. But when our thoughts and feelings are intense, we are not reflecting on this—or even on the facts. We are responding to the primitive, and powerful, alarm in our head. *We are hijacked.*

When we are jealous, our threat-detection system is activated. We look for any sign that our partner might be interested in someone else—or that someone else is interested in him or her. We view other people as imminent threats, and our partner's thoughts and feelings become potential signs of betrayal. Our minds are determined to find clues—no matter how small and subtle they might be.

In this chapter, we will explore how our minds operate when we are in Jealousy Mode, which is a combination of thoughts, feelings, behaviors, strategies, and communications that often *operate together*. Jealousy Mode is triggered by our threat-detection system when it determines that something might be going on. Once we are caught up in the Jealousy Mode, we have a difficult time stepping away from it. Our emotions escalate. When Jealousy Mode is activated and running the show, it has dramatic effects, including taking things personally, mindreading, predicting catastrophes, applying impossible standards and rules to our relationship, activating worry as a way to cope with the unknown, and dwelling on all the negatives—imaginary or real—that our mind can dredge up. As a result, we become anxious, agitated, angry, and depressed. In this chapter, we'll consider how our predispositions may escalate our jealousy, maintain it, and lead us to take actions that we might regret later.

There are four parts of the jealous mind: *core beliefs, rulebooks, biased thinking,* and *worry and rumination.*[25] Each component reinforces the others, keeping us locked into a system that does the following: maintains, and elaborates on, initial threat detection; magnifies the importance of events; directs us to confirm our fears; and keeps us stuck imagining what could happen or what we think has happened. Let's take a closer look at each of these components.

Core Beliefs

We have core beliefs about ourselves and others that direct our jealous thinking. Core beliefs are generalities that describe how we think about things. They create habitual biases that we often are not aware of. For example, a core belief about the self might be, "I am unlovable"—not interesting, attractive, desirable, or able to maintain the love of other people. This core belief is the lens through which you see the world, but you seldom realize that you are wearing a lens. Imagine wearing dark sunglasses all the time, which make everything seem dimmer and darker than they are. If you don't realize that you have these glasses on, you end up thinking that the world is always dark. That is what a core belief does. It's a lens that biases the way you see things.

You may have put on your jealousy lens. You see everything through that lens, and very little lightness or positivity can get through to you. You are locked into your own perspective.

When Beliefs Appear as Facts

We can mistake our beliefs and thoughts for facts. It happens frequently. Here's a scenario that shows how this works. Say you are in a strange city and it's late at night. You are alone, walking back to your hotel. There is no one else on the street. Suddenly, you hear two men walking at a fast pace behind you. You think, "These guys are going to mug me—they might even kill me." Your thought of danger leads you to become extremely anxious and afraid, you walk faster, and worry that you might not make it.

But wait. What if you had a different thought? What if you thought, "Those are two guys from the conference. They are probably heading back to the same hotel." You don't feel anxious, you might even feel relieved. You take your time.

In both cases, the initial facts are the same—being on the street, late at night, with two strangers walking more quickly behind you. What differs is your *interpretation* of the facts, whether it is dangerous or not dangerous. Our interpretations can be true or false.

When we are anxious, angry, or sad *we often treat our thoughts as if they are facts*. The thoughts appear in your head and you then reach conclusions: your partner must be interested in someone else, he or she will betray you, you are no longer loved or special. But not all thoughts are true, and you won't know until you check out the facts.

Is a Core Belief a Fact?

Imagine if I said to you, "I think I am a zebra." You would look at me in disbelief, thinking I am insane. I then insist: "I believe, 100 percent, that I am a zebra." How do we figure out whether my confidence is merited? We look at the facts. I look in the mirror and I am astounded to see I don't have any stripes. I don't look like a horse.

When we are angry or anxious, we often treat our thoughts as if they are true. Our confidence that we are correct becomes the proof. But believing something to be true doesn't make it so, and our confidence is not really evidence.

Identify the core beliefs floating around in your mind that contribute to jealousy. Then look at facts and logic to determine the truth. You may be right—maybe your partner is planning on cheating—or you may not be right.

Core beliefs that contribute to jealousy are negative thoughts that we treat as absolutely true. Here are some common ones.

- If you have a core belief that you are not lovable, then you might fear that your partner will find someone who is more interesting or attractive than you.

- You might believe you are not able to take care of yourself: you need someone else or you think you cannot be happy on your own. This core belief may lead you to profoundly fear losing a partner who takes care of you or is a companion.

- Some people have a core belief that they are special and unique—superior to others. With this belief, you view others as threats to your status and think, "If my partner is interested in someone else, then this means that I am not special and unique."

Core Beliefs About Other People

We can also have core beliefs about other people. One core belief is that people are judgmental. This can lead to jealousy because you believe that any negative judgment your partner may have will threaten the relationship. You hold the impossible standard that your partner has to like everything about you. In addition, this focus may lead you to believe that your partner—and other people—are constantly thinking that you are inferior. With a core belief about the harshness of others, your self-esteem becomes fragile as you assume that if someone doesn't like something about you, then you must be inferior or undesirable. Your self-esteem goes up and down, depending on how you think other people are evaluating you in any given moment.

Looking for Confirmation Rather Than Facts

A consequence of core beliefs is a confirmation bias.[26] This is our automatic tendency to seek out information that confirms our preexisting beliefs. We are seldom conscious of this bias— it's our minds on autopilot, searching the environment for information that proves we are right.

So if you have the core belief that you are boring, then you will automatically see evidence of it when someone yawns. If someone changes the topic, it means that what you're saying has nothing valuable to contribute. You only see information consistent with your current belief.

Memory is also directed toward information that confirms our core beliefs. When people are depressed, they selectively recall failure, rejection, and disappointment. Their memories are directed by current moods and negative beliefs about themselves. The same is true with our core beliefs about ourselves—we selectively remember information that is consistent with an idea that we are not lovable or interesting or able to maintain relationships. It's not that we want to suffer—this happens simply because our mind is running in automatic mode. Later in the book, you'll learn techniques that you can use to slow down your thinking and examine the full range of evidence in a less biased way.

The same confirmation bias operates when we think of other people. For example, if you think that others are untrustworthy, you selectively notice and recall information that confirms that other people lie, cheat, and manipulate. I have heard both men and women express core beliefs that "Men can't be trusted" and "Women can't be trusted." Of course you can find evidence of both men and women to confirm your negative belief, but you can also find a lot of evidence that argues against it.

The problem is that we tend to focus on whatever confirms our preexisting beliefs. Core beliefs are overly general (men can't be trusted), rigid (they are applied relentlessly), and directed by confirmation bias (seeking out information consistent with the belief). Consider this simple example of confirmation bias in jealousy. Let's say you have a core belief that people can't be trusted and your mind is off and running to confirm this. You can engage in mindreading ("My wife is lying," "She is interested in someone else," or "She finds me boring"). You have selective attention to the slightest detail of possibility: the yoga mat is at home, therefore she is lying. Then you might notice that she is looking at her boss and infer, through more mindreading, that she is interested in having an affair with him. You start predicting the future with almost no evidence, while discounting any signs that she is committed to you, because that is not consistent with your core belief that she—like others—cannot be trusted.

Example of Confirmation Bias in Jealousy

Core Belief:	People are not trustworthy.
Look for Clues:	"My wife said she was at yoga, but I saw her mat at home."
Discount Anything Positive About the Relationship:	"She kisses me goodnight, and every night I wonder who else she's kissed that day."
Magnify Negatives:	"I can't stop thinking about the way my wife was looking at her boss."

What happens when a core belief comes up against information that is not consistent with the belief? For example, you find that you can trust your female doctor. You will *discount* the new evidence by thinking something like, "There are always exceptions to the rule, but everyone knows that women can't be trusted."

We further maintain our core beliefs by relying on *anecdotes*. Anecdotes are memorable—we pay attention to them, we remember them. "Don't you recall how our friend Susan's husband cheated on her?" These anecdotes are often quite vivid. You can form a picture in your mind, you might know the person, and your story has a beginning, a middle, and an end. But one anecdote is not evidence for the whole world, is it?

Our minds did not evolve to think about percentages or base rates—that is, the percentage of people who are faithful and trustworthy. We put much more emphasis on information that has a story and a picture. That's why the news loves to show dramatic videos of things happening. Who wants to look at a graph when you can watch a car crashing into a wall?

We also rely on *biased information*—information that is memorable, has an anecdote, and seems personally relevant to us. It's like googling the word "accident" and up comes 418,000,000 results. So we conclude that we should be strapped to our chairs with helmets and never leave our houses. We don't google "safety" or "likelihood of an accident." So our results will bias us toward the belief that the world is dangerous. The same thing happens with our jealousy and our core beliefs. We keep proving ourselves right.

Where Do These Beliefs Come From?

Most of our core beliefs about ourselves are established during childhood. Here are some common ones that fuel jealousy.

- If we are surrounded by people who are untrustworthy, invalidating, and deceitful, we are likely to develop a core belief that people cannot be trusted.

- If we are told that appearances are everything, then we may form a core belief that being attractive to our partner is the only thing holding the relationship together. This can lead to jealousy when we think that our partner finds someone else attractive because we must be the most attractive person to him or her and, in addition, that our partner must think that we are the *only attractive person*.

- Lack of attention from our parents can lead to the core belief that we are not interesting. We can internalize the idea that we are not interesting or lovable, which causes us to distrust the people we get involved with.

Think about your core beliefs about yourself and other people. Are there any significant patterns? Can you recall how your childhood experiences, or experiences across the entire span of your life, may have reinforced certain beliefs about yourself and other people? Here's an example.

Gwen's father was usually busy at work—even when he was at home—and he had little time for her. As a child, she didn't realize that her father really loved her and thought she was smart and creative. But he was compulsive about work, dedicated to his research, and anxious that he was falling behind. As a result, she found herself reliving this scene with others, seeking out approval from men who were unavailable, ungiving, and often secretive.

Your Core Beliefs

Reflecting on your core beliefs about yourself and others may help you understand which factors can fuel your jealousy at times. Consider the following questions in terms of your childhood and significant adult relationships.

- Was there emphasis on being physically attractive, powerful, rich, successful, entertaining, or interesting?

- Did you feel pressure to be some way, or do something, in order to be accepted?

- Did you think they couldn't just love you for who you are?

- Did you feel that people were not always there for you?

- Did your parents invalidate your feelings?

- Did you fear that they might even leave?

- Did you think that they were disappointed in you?

- Were there threats of abandonment? Even subtle threats?

- Did you sense that the relationship between your parents was problematic?

We all have vulnerabilities, we all have imperfect childhoods and imperfect parents, and we all have imperfect relationships.

But some of us become more hurt, disappointed, or simply confused about things. These painful experiences can leave a mark on us. They linger on in the jealous mind.

Rule-Books

The second part of the jealous mind is having rule-books. These are rules, ideas, and assumptions that we have about ourselves and other people. They are often framed this way: "*If* this happens, *then* that needs to happen." For example, I have a rule so I don't get wet when it rains. *If* there is a high probability of rain, *then* I carry an umbrella.

Rule-books seem to operate automatically, almost like a thinking reflex that leads us to immediately believe something before we have time to look at the facts. Rule-books might be lying under the surface, but we can reflect on patterns of anxiety, anger, and sadness to see whether we have rules that contribute to jealousy.

Your rules may make you think that, *if* you follow these guidelines, *then* you will be able to predict and control what will happen. They may seem important to you because you assume that they will protect you. You may think that your rules are realistic, ensuring that you won't be duped, that you can predict what will happen, that you will be able to control things, and that you might be able to get out of a situation before it's too late. But your rules may also lead you to overreact, jump to conclusions, and undermine yourself.

These rules apply to other people, ourselves, and our relationships. We can have them about how people should relate to us, think about us, and feel about us. They can tell us what we think we need to do. And they can fuel jealousy. Let's take a closer look at some of the implicit rules and assumptions that can reside in the jealous mind. Consider the following rules we commonly have, and see whether any apply to you.

Rules About Others

- I shouldn't trust others because they will betray me

- If someone disappoints me in something, then I can never trust them again

- I need to know everything about my partner in order to trust him or her

- If my partner really loved me, he or she would never find anyone else interesting or attractive

- I can't rely on other people to be there for me

- Men, or women, are always looking for a better option

Rules About Ourselves

- I should be the most attractive person—all the time

- I should get approval from my partner for almost everything I do

- I need to entertain others or they will find me boring

- I need to have a relationship in order to be happy

- I can never disappoint anyone

- I should be happy and secure all the time

Rules About Relationships

- We should be intensely happy, all the time

- My partner should tell me everything that he or she is thinking and feeling

- Our sex life should be amazing—always intense and spontaneous

- We should never have arguments

- My partner should always be available to me

- I should always know exactly where my partner is, what he or she is doing, and who he or she is with

- We should never have secrets

- Relationships are either all good, or all bad

What are the consequences of these rules? Let's look at this one: "If my partner really loved me, he or she would never find anyone else interesting or attractive." Here are some questions to ponder to assess how realistic this rule is.

- Does it make sense that you would be the only person in the world that your partner found attractive?

- Do you find other people attractive?

- Does this mean that you cannot be trusted?

- Do you find other people interesting?

- Does finding someone else interesting or attractive mean that you will betray your partner?

No one will live up to the expectations behind this rule. So having it will guarantee that you will feel disappointed, insecure, and jealous. How about a different thought, one that might be more realistic and adaptive: "There are many people who are also attractive and interesting, but that doesn't mean my partner doesn't love me or that he or she will betray me." Consider the advantages of this new thought. Is it realistic?

Let's look at this rule: "I need to have a relationship in order to be happy." What are the consequences of this rule for you?

- Because it implies that you can't be happy without a relationship, does it make you more vulnerable to anxiety and jealousy?

- Does it make you fear losing the relationship you have even more?

- Does it ensure misery for you if you are single?

- Is it really true? Were you ever happy—even for a moment—before the current relationship?

As much as we may love our partner and derive great satisfaction from our relationship, is it really *essential* that we have this particular relationship? We may think and feel it is essential, but it is very likely that you have had meaning, satisfaction, and happiness before this relationship. Therefore, it is likely that even if this relationship didn't work out, you would be able to thrive again.

Let's consider the consequences for another rule: "I should always know exactly where my partner is, what he or she is doing, and who he or she is with."

- Does this rule contribute to your anxiety, jealousy, and helplessness?

- Can you really know, for sure, exactly what your partner is doing?

- Does your partner always know what you are doing?

- Are you assuming that, if you don't know, then your partner is betraying you?

- If your partner didn't know where you were today, does that mean you are betraying him or her?

Here are questions to ask about one more rule: "My partner should tell me everything that he or she is thinking and feeling."

- Are you assuming that private thoughts and feelings are dangerous?

- What is the evidence that they are dangerous?

- Don't you have some thoughts and feelings—some memories, perhaps some fantasies—that you don't always share?

- Does not sharing them mean that no one can trust you?

- Does demanding to know everything make you less trusting, lead you to interrogate your partner, or start arguments?

- What would the danger be if you were to accept some privacy for both of you?

If your rules demand perfection, absolute certainty, total happiness, and satisfaction all the time—then you are dooming yourself to frustration, misery, and jealousy. Reflect on your pattern of jealousy and frustration. Ask yourself what rules you are using. Would you be better off with more acceptance, less perfectionism, and more flexibility? Do you know people who have less demanding and intrusive rules? Are they always miserable?

Biased Thinking

A third part of our thinking style includes common biases in thinking that can lead to distortions. These are thoughts that come to you automatically—spontaneously—as if they are thinking reflexes biased toward distrust and jealousy.

It may be that your thought turns out to be true—maybe your partner is thinking about someone else and, it's possible, that your partner might cheat on you. But the important thing to notice here is that you may be biased toward these threats, even when they are not accurate. Here are twelve common biases in thinking that might contribute to your jealousy. Take a look and see whether any are familiar to you.

Mindreading: You assume that you know what your partner, or others, are thinking without having sufficient evidence of their thoughts. "He thinks she's sexy" or "She's after my husband."

Fortunetelling: You predict the future negatively. Things will get worse, or there is danger ahead. "He will run off with someone else" or "She will be unfaithful to me."

Catastrophizing: You believe that what has happened, or could happen, is so awful and unbearable that you won't be able to stand it. "It would devastate me if I were betrayed" or "It is the end of everything between us because he finds another woman appealing."

Labeling: You assign global, negative traits to yourself and others. "I'm boring" or "He's a cheat."

Discounting Positives: You claim that the positive things about you, or your relationship, are trivial. "Just because she says she loves me doesn't mean she won't cheat on me" or "Even though there are a lot of good things in our relationship, I still can't trust him."

Negative Filtering: You focus almost exclusively on the negatives and seldom notice the positives in your relationship. "We haven't had sex in a couple of weeks" or "We had an argument so that means that things are really bad and he might leave me."

Overgeneralizing: On the basis of a single incident, you perceive a global pattern of negatives. "She is flirtatious whenever we are out with other people" or "He seems to have lost interest in me because last night we didn't talk much."

Dichotomous Thinking: You view events or people in all-or-nothing terms. "Nothing seems to be going well in our relationship" or "She never seems interested in being affectionate" or "We are always arguing."

Shoulds: You interpret events in terms of how things should be, rather than simply focusing on what is. "We should be excited and turned on to each other all the time" or "My girlfriend should never find other people attractive and interesting."

Personalizing: You take things personally in your relationship, as if anything done by your partner, or others, reflects on you. "If she finds another man interesting, then that means I must be boring" or "He was caught up surfing the internet—he is losing interest in me."

Blaming: You focus on the other person as the source of your negative feelings, and you refuse to take responsibility for changing yourself. "The reason I am upset is that she doesn't give me the attention I need" or "He is trying to make me jealous by talking to another woman."

Emotional Reasoning: You let your feelings guide your interpretation of reality. "I feel anxious, so that means that my partner is up to something" or "I feel like things are boring, so that means my partner will look for someone more interesting and exciting." These automatic, negative thoughts feed your rules or assumptions: "If she likes someone else, then she will betray me." This confirms a core belief: "I am unlovable."

Here's how this might work. It is possible to have an *accurate* thought that your partner is thinking of another man that she finds attractive. Because you have a rule that "If my partner finds other men attractive, then she will betray me," you get anxious and angry. Your accurate thought may feed into a core belief about yourself: that you are inadequate, less attractive, boring, or defective in some way. You become depressed and self-protective.

Kevin is planning on going to a party with Stacey, his girl-friend, and her ex-boyfriend will be there. He thinks:

- "Stacey will find Allen to be really sexy" (fortunetelling, mindreading)

- "If she finds him sexy, then it means she thinks I'm inferior" (personalizing, mindreading)

- "I can't stand for her to think other men are sexy" (catastrophizing)

- "I know Stacey broke up with Allen, and that she claims she loves me, but I can't count on that" (discounting the positive)

- "If she left me, it would be the worst thing in the world for me" (catastrophizing)

You can see how Kevin goes through a cascade of negative thoughts that lead him to conclude that she might dump him and go back to Allen, and that if this happened his life would not be worth living. Look closely at how your negative, biased thoughts may contribute to your jealousy.

Worry and Rumination

A fourth aspect of jealous thinking is relying on negative predictions about the future (worry) and dwelling on negatives from the past or present (rumination). Worry and rumination are similar processes and involve getting stuck on a negative thought.[27] This is when we get hijacked by our thoughts—the thought appears and we are taken along for a ride.

You might have the negative thought, "He finds that other woman attractive," and you could respond by dismissing the thought as irrelevant, or you might accept the idea that we all find many people attractive. With these responses, you don't get stuck on the thought—you let it go. But if you worry about it, your mind spins around like a wheel stuck in the mud—the more you think about what might happen, the more negatives come up. You begin thinking about how your partner might be more interested in someone else, you get more anxious and angry, and you can't get the thought out of your head. If you ruminate, you recall a negative in the past—"I remember that at a party last month he was talking to Angie a lot"—and you dwell on it, continually bringing it up in your head.

Because we generally feel much worse when we worry or ruminate, why do we do it? We worry because we think it might help us.[28] Worry is usually about "What if?" while rumination is often about "Why?" When we are jealous, we think, "I need to worry about the future in order to be prepared and not get caught off guard." Or we believe we need to ruminate because we will be able to figure things out and solve the problem. In this way, worry and rumination seem like strategies for coping with threats of rejection, betrayal, and abandonment. Jealousy can even be thought of as angry, agitated worry.[29]

The problem with repetitive worry is that it eventually leads to more anxiety and depression. It's like opening a file cabinet filled with the worst things that you can imagine and then rummaging through it for hours. You are *partnering with negatives*, aligning your thoughts with them. It's like your moods, your thoughts, and your reality are all the same. You have a hard time stepping back, observing that a thought is just a thought or a mood that will pass. You are not only likely to feel much worse, but you are also likely to miss out on the positives in your life at the present moment. You can't enjoy your present life when you focus on imaginary negatives.

Another problem is that you often worry because you cannot accept *uncertainty*—not knowing for sure really bothers you. You think uncertainty means that something bad will happen, that it is a sign of something being hidden from you. Perhaps most importantly, you think that it's *possible* to get certainty.[30] You might believe that, if you keep thinking about it, then you will gain absolute certainty.

But there is no certainty in an uncertain world. It is a fruitless and impossible quest that locks you into a repetitive, negative cycle. Each time you come up with the idea "I think I can trust him," you ask another question: "But can I be absolutely sure?" Then you reject any positives and go back to worry. In chapters 6, 7, and 8, we will look at a number of powerful techniques that you can use immediately to set aside these worries and get on with your life.

Rumination, or dwelling on the negative, is similar to worry but tends to focus on past events or asking yourself questions that never seem to have an answer, such as "Why is this happening?" or "When will I ever feel better?" People who ruminate are more likely to get depressed and stay depressed. When we ruminate, we often believe we can figure things out, get all the information, make sense of everything, and get the complete picture.[31] We keep spinning around, asking ourselves—or our partner—unanswerable questions, then rejecting any answers we get as incomplete, unsatisfying, and even deceptive. Ruminating prevents us from participating in our lives: we do not enjoy what is going on right in front of us, we are seldom in the present moment where life is happening, and we are dredging up negative, unanswerable questions.[32]

Putting the Jealous Mind Together

I began this chapter by describing the Jealousy Mode, and the jealous mind is one part of that mode. The other parts—which we will soon discuss—include your emotions, your behaviors, the ways you communicate, and your coping strategies. So let's put all aspects of the jealous mind together to help you understand the way you think first.

We each start with some core beliefs about ourselves and other people. Let's say my core beliefs are that I am not good enough to be lovable and that others cannot be trusted. This is then coupled with rule-books, which say that "I have to be perfect to be loved" and "My partner has to like everything about me." The idea is that *if* I try to be perfect, *then* my basic unlovability will not emerge and lead to rejection. My rule-book about others says, "Other people are a threat to my relationship" or "If my partner finds someone else to be attractive or interesting, then she will betray me." So I start looking for clues, discounting positives about my partner, and worrying about the future.

Because I start with the core belief that "I am not good enough to be lovable," the assumption follows that "I must be perfect for my partner to stay with me." So I selectively focus on my imperfections, exaggerate the importance of them, and assume that this means my relationship is in jeopardy. Then I engage in mindreading ("My partner thinks I am boring"), personalizing ("She yawned because she has lost interest"), and fortunetelling ("She will find someone else"). The Jealousy Mode keeps me locked into reinforcing my jealousy, testing my partner, doubting myself, and increasing my anxiety and anger. It's like stepping on the gas pedal and acting surprised that I am accelerating off a cliff.

Another way of looking at our own jealous mind is to start with the negative, biased thinking—our automatic thoughts—and then work down to our core assumptions. So, let's imagine that I think my partner is bored with me right now. Why would that bother me? (After all, all of us are boring some of the time.) Well, it bothers me because I then activate my rule-book, which says, "I must be perfect to keep my partner's interest." It is the rule-book and the assumption that give intensity and importance to the negative thought "I sound boring." Perhaps if you didn't have that rule-book, you could accept being boring some of the time.

It's helpful to also look at why it would be so upsetting if my partner left me for someone else. Because I think I am unlovable—boring and unattractive—she would confirm those beliefs by leaving. Whereas if I thought I was interesting and attractive, I might instead think, "While it would be very unpleasant if she betrayed me, because I have qualities other women might want, I would find someone else."

Once my core beliefs about myself and others are activated, my rule-books are also activated. This leads me to activate my threat detection—looking for clues ("She wasn't actually at her mother's house"), engaging in mindreading ("Who is she thinking about?"), or taking things personally ("She is silent because she is bored with me"). I then activate the coping strategies we will soon discuss—worry, rumination, interrogating, testing, provoking, withdrawing—to find out what is really going on. My partner withdraws further from me, becomes angry with me, and this fuels my belief that things are falling apart. All of the thoughts, rules, and beliefs lead me to coping strategies that only make matters worse. Jealousy Mode has taken over and I am at risk of ruining my relationship.

Core Beliefs →	Rule-Books →	Biased Thinking
Self: "I am unlovable."	"I must be perfect to be loved." "My partner has to like everything about me."	I focus on my negatives. I discount any of my positives.
Others: "I can't trust people in intimate relationships."	"Other people are a threat to my relationship." "If my partner finds someone else to be attractive or interesting, she will betray me."	Mindreading: "My partner finds him appealing." Personalizing: "I must be losing my appeal." Fortunetelling: "She will betray me."

Hijacked by Emotions

Do you ever feel like Sarah? Her jealousy seems to overwhelm her at times.

> "When Kent is gone on a business trip, I feel so lonely, so desperate, I just can't stand it. I keep imagining that he is flirting with other women and then I feel this rush of anxiety, like I am going to go crazy. I don't know what to do. It's like this feeling comes over me, in the pit of my stomach, and I don't know how to get rid of it. I don't have words to describe this feeling—it's like a terror. My heart is beating so rapidly, I want to cry. Sometimes I cry. I feel that I am losing control."

Sarah's experience is not unusual. She feels overwhelmed with her feelings and realizes that she has so many different feelings. She thinks they are so intense that she will go insane. She fears that if she doesn't get rid of these feelings, they will escalate, get worse, and lead her to lose control. She feels bewildered, helpless, and overwhelmed.

Jealousy is not simply being plagued by a set of thoughts or assumptions. In fact, your thought "My partner is interested in someone else" may be only part of the struggle going on in your mind. It's more likely you are bothered by all the emotions that go with the thoughts. These include:

- Anxiety that comes from uncertainty about what is happening and fear of loss or betrayal

- Anger that you might be manipulated, humiliated, and treated unfairly

- Confusion because you don't know for sure what is going on

- Ambivalence about your relationship, because you recognize that you love someone who might hurt you

These emotions may come to you in waves—one after another, sometimes ebbing, sometimes flowing, sometimes making you feel numb. You may think, at times, that you have no control over these emotions because they are so intense, so immediate, and so automatic. It's hard to imagine that these emotions might be temporary, that a few hours from now your emotions might be different.

When you are in Jealous Mode, you feel carried away by these emotions—as if there is nothing that you can do except follow them, be captured by them, and surrender to them. It's as if the present-moment emotion rules you. You may lash out, withdraw, threaten, or say things that you later regret. It is these emotions, you think, that have driven you to say and do things that you may later wish you had never said or done.

This experience is Emotional Hijacking, and it is frightening because you believe that you are a victim of overwhelming emotions. Sometimes it seems that your emotions don't make any sense, that what provoked a jealous rage turns out to be so minor when the reality eventually emerges later. Sometimes you think that, if you don't understand why your emotions are so intense, it means you are helpless: "What I don't understand, I can't control." Plus, when you experience these emotions, you think that they will go on forever—they will escalate to overwhelm you. You respond by saying to yourself, "I can't stand having these feelings," and you think that you have to get rid of them—*immediately*. And this Emotional Hijacking of your mind and heart leads you to interrogate, attack, withdraw, and threaten. See whether any of these thoughts about emotions are familiar to you.

- I can't stand these feelings

- My feelings are going to drive me insane

- No one else understands me

- I shouldn't have these feelings

- Other people don't have my feelings

- Intense emotions are dangerous

- There must be something wrong with me that I feel this way

- I am embarrassed about these feelings

- If I don't get rid of these feelings immediately, they will escalate

- These feelings will go on and on and on

- I must do something right now to get rid of these feelings

- I can't accept these feelings

As you read these statements, try to be honest about how you think. They reflect a wide range of problematic beliefs about emotion, including beliefs that your emotions (like anger, anxiety, sadness, and helplessness) are out of control, will last indefinitely, are different from the emotions of other people, don't make sense, and have to be eliminated immediately.

Your emotions are blasting like a fire alarm that signals a catastrophe.

But emotions are experiences that are going on inside you. The fire alarm is not the same thing as the fire. The emotions are crying out. Soon you will see how you can: acknowledge every emotion that you have; validate your right to have whatever feelings that you feel; accept them for the moment; and step back and examine your thoughts, your feelings, your relationship, the events that are occurring—or that you suspect to be occurring—and the options available to you.

For many of us, there is nothing so horrifying as Emotional Hijacking. You don't want to feel that your heart and mind can be taken over, and that your emotions can override your daily experience. But you can't eliminate your emotions and you can't live without them. Certain things come with the territory. Where there is love, there is always the possibility of jealousy.

You have seen so far how jealousy has evolved, how it is universal, how we find it in babies and animals. You are not alone. These emotions are intense—but like all emotions, they subside with time. It doesn't seem that way when you are hijacked. But what if you knew that whatever you feel in this moment, you will not feel at a later moment? What if you knew that the things provoking your jealousy, right now, will be things you will feel indifferent about at a later time? Reflecting on past experiences of this is hard to access in the middle of Emotional Hijacking, but take a moment now and try to recall things that bothered you a few years ago. Has the intensity of your feelings about them subsided?

In part III, we will review a wide range of valuable and powerful techniques that you can use to help you cope with the intensity of Emotional Hijacking. We will develop a plan so that you can identify the triggers, step away from the situation, and acknowledge that the feelings are in the present moment. Then you can consider options for disentangling yourself from the intensity and acting in your interest—not based on your emotions.

You can start by validating your jealousy—it is a painful, overwhelming, difficult experience. You are not alone. This book was written for you, to help you understand that these emotions are part of being human, and to help you see that another part of being human is being able to step away from emotion, not act on reflex, and keep options in front of you.

When you are hijacked by jealousy, you may think that you are on a roller coaster, terrified and screaming as you rush down into the depths of your emotions. You think that this will go on forever or that you are going to crash. It's like a catastrophe is exploding in front of you. But there are three ways to ride a roller coaster: go along for the ride, slow it down, or get off. You have a choice.

In the next chapter, we will review some of the problematic things that you say or do when you have these jealous thoughts and feelings. I call them "strategies" because you may think that these responses to your jealousy will help you, or that you have no choice because you feel so overwhelmed. Then, in chapter 6, we will look at how you can step away for a moment, step back, accept the feelings for the present, and live alongside the feelings and thoughts that previously hijacked you and carried you away.

The emotions and thoughts will pass. But you will still be here.

Chapter 5

Jealous Strategies That Drive Your Partner Away

"I thought he was probably flirting with Lilly on his business trip, comparing me to her, and I was just so pissed off I couldn't stand thinking about him. So when he got home I went after him. I was so angry, I was afraid that he might dump me. I began accusing him of having an affair, telling him he was a lying bastard, yelling at him. He just looked bewildered. Then he said, Sharon, Lilly wasn't even there. She had to cancel her business trip because her kid was sick. I felt like I was crazy. And, I have to admit, I have done a lot of things I feel guilty about. I checked the GPS in our car to see where he was driving. I wondered if he might be going over to see Lilly when he left the house for several hours. I followed him to the health club because I knew that she belonged to a health club—I wasn't sure which one, though. I get these jealous feelings and I just think I need to do something. I need to find out. I must be crazy."

Like Sharon, you may be having a hard time accepting that you feel jealous, anxious, and angry because you believe that these feelings will last a long time, they will escalate, and they will overwhelm you. You are afraid to let these feelings happen, so you think you need to do something. It's like you fear that you will drown in water, so you frantically slap at the water in a panic. But you begin to sink.

In this chapter, we will look at a wide range of problematic strategies that you use. While I call these "strategies," I don't want to imply that you are deliberately choosing these behaviors—they may seem to occur automatically. In fact, you may think that you have no choice in the matter. You might even think, "Of course I did that and said that. *I was jealous.*" But you can get to a point in which you recognize that you are having an intense feeling. Then you can step away from the feeling, allow yourself a few minutes to reflect, and consider what you are about to do. Feeling is different from acting.

We have looked at worry and rumination, a strategy that you might use to anticipate what is going on, predict the possible infidelity, and try to control things before they get out of hand. In later chapters, I will outline a wide range of techniques and adaptive strategies that you can immediately start using, but first let's review some of the problematic strategies that you might be using now.

With any strategy I describe, I am going to ask you to consider both the advantages and the disadvantages of using it. I am not saying you should never do any of these things—only that you might want to consider the trade-offs, risks, and alternatives. Keep in mind that each response or strategy you have is a choice, so you want to be able to think about possible consequences and, later, think about alternatives to these choices.[33]

Interrogation

One strategy is to interrogate your partner. You question every detail about what happened. You want to know all the facts, and you think that the more information you are able to get out of your partner, the better things will be for you. You want to know *for sure* what is happening—and you think your partner is holding back.

Your questions might be subtle, so you can see how your partner responds: "So, did you have a good time with the people at that party? Anyone I know there?" Or your questions could be more direct: "Was Lilly there? Did you talk with her?" or "Who was sitting next to you?" Sometimes the interrogation can sound accusatory: "Are you seeing someone?" You might ask a series of questions, looking for more details, asking the same question but with different words—very much like an attorney.

The more you question your partner, the more defensive he or she may become, telling you, "I haven't done anything wrong." You treat this defensiveness as evidence that they are hiding something. You keep at it, question after question. You have set up a prosecutor and defendant game, where you are both prosecutor and judge. No matter what your partner says, you find them guilty.

What are the costs and benefits of this approach? The costs include your partner's growing defensiveness, more arguments, and more distrust building between the two of you. Your partner feels attacked; you feel ignored and even manipulated. Continual interrogations might even lead your partner to decide not to share things with you, because the questioning leads to escalation of arguments, stonewalling (deliberate withdrawal or evasion), or both. In some cases, the interrogation may become so unpleasant that the relationship disintegrates to the point of a breakup. The relationship ends, not because of infidelity, but because of constant arguments that arise from constant questioning.

You might consider some of the possible benefits of asking a lot of questions. Perhaps your partner is not telling you the truth and is hiding things from you. If your partner completely stonewalls and refuses to discuss anything, it may be possible that he or she is trying to keep you from the truth. For example, one woman told me that her partner would disappear overnight and then refuse to tell her where he was. She eventually broke it off with him.

Looking for Clues

As we discussed in the last chapter, a jealous mind gets set off by a belief that something is being hidden from you, and that your partner is trying to get away with something—flirtations, secret meetings or communications, possibly an affair. But at this stage, you don't know. So you begin searching for any small sign that your partner is unfaithful or interested in someone else. We saw how Sharon would interrogate, search for clues, check her husband's GPS—but each time coming up only with more fuel for her checking and interrogating. Here are some more examples.

- You watch your partner's appearance: Is he or she looking more dressed up, more sexually provocative, more concerned with appearance?

- You wonder why he or she hasn't done that in the past— *for you!*

- You might sniff his or her clothing looking for fragrances of perfume, cologne, or smoke (when he or she is not a smoker).

- You wonder where your partner has been, so you search the GPS in the car or you try to get access to his or her phone.

- You look on social media to find out who your partner is friending on Facebook. Is he or she sending photos to anyone?

- If your partner is an hour late, you wonder whether it indicates that he or she has been out with someone.

- If your partner has been less interested in sex recently, you wonder whether it's evidence that he or she has found someone else.

- You might notice that your partner has been especially nice to you, so you wonder whether that is a manipulation to hide what is really going on.

The disadvantage of continually looking for clues is that you are starting with an assumption about infidelity—and then trying to prove that you are right. It's possible that anything less than perfection from your partner could be taken as evidence. You may selectively focus on small, insignificant details and blow them up into major issues. You engage in mindreading, without sufficient reason to claim you actually know what your partner is thinking. Because anything can be taken as a clue, you discount and ignore any of your partner's positive behaviors. The more you look for clues, the less available you become for intimacy, relaxation, and pleasure—further alienating yourself from your partner.

Of course, there are some possible benefits of looking for clues. Perhaps you will discover something that will unravel the truth and you can know, for sure, that your partner is cheating. Ironically, there is no way of unraveling the truth that your partner is faithful, because your biased search for clues discounts any positive behavior as something insignificant or even as a manipulation to hide the truth. All of this is a matter of balance and proportion. There is no way that searching for clues can turn out positively if it becomes a major preoccupation. You need to ask yourself whether this is really working for you—or whether this is creating more conflict, more distrust, and more jealousy.

Looking for Signs That Other People Are Interested in Your Partner

You scan the social environment to see whether someone else is interested in flirting with your partner. This is a version of looking for clues—but here you look for clues in the behavior of *other people*. You begin treating other people as competitors, or even suspects. "Is that woman looking at my husband? Is there something going on between them?" "Is that man smiling at my wife because he knows something that I don't know?" You find yourself suspicious that your partner is talking with someone else—enjoying himself or herself, laughing. You feel enraged if someone touches your partner because it suggests that the other person feels some right to trespass on what you feel is rightfully *yours*. You might be really upset if you are at a party and your partner dances with someone else: "Shouldn't she only be dancing with me? After all, she came here with me!"

This strategy was something that Sharon used quite often when she was out in public with her husband. If they were at a restaurant, she would look at how the waitress talked to him. Was she smiling at him? Was she talking with him more than with Sharon? Were there other women in the restaurant looking in his direction?

The disadvantage of this strategy is that socializing can become a competition between you and other people—often people you don't even know. You will be less likely to enjoy time with your partner because you will be looking for threats from everywhere. In some cases, you might begin preventing the two of you from socializing with other people.

You might believe that this strategy has some advantages. You may think you will be able to catch the secretive flirting, or the people who might threaten your relationship, and then confront your partner with this information to keep things from getting worse. The problem, of course, is that you are likely to have a lot of false alarms, which will lead to an escalation of conflict that might, ironically, drive you and your partner apart. Is this strategy actually helping you?

Pouting and Withdrawing

With this strategy, you silently and subtly decrease your interactions with your partner. You say to yourself, "Let him try to figure out what is going on." You don't show any affection, don't talk as much, don't laugh anymore. You withdraw: sometimes you aren't around and sometimes you don't respond to his or her calls and texts. You want your partner to know how it feels to miss you, you want to punish him or her, but you don't want to admit that this is your intention. When your partner asks you what is wrong, you deny that there is anything wrong. After all, if he or she really cared, really loved you, "She would just know what's wrong." But she doesn't know. You get to make your partner feel bad—maybe, you hope, make him or her feel guilty—and you set up a test to see whether he or she really cares about you. And your partner fails the test.

This is what Sharon would do to express her anger with her husband. It allowed her to be hostile—by being passive-aggressive—and she didn't have to openly acknowledge that she was hostile. When her husband would ask her what was wrong, she would deny that anything was wrong, which would confuse him and lead him to withdraw.

The disadvantage of pouting and withdrawing is that it is hard to see how your relationship gets better with this strategy. If you are afraid that your partner is losing interest, pouting and withdrawing is even more likely to drive him or her away. The idea of testing, to see whether your partner cares, might backfire because they might view your behavior as unreasonable—and unrewarding.

On the other hand, you might believe that pulling away from your partner will help you find out whether he or she really cares about you. It could be possible for him or her to initiate contact and try to get closer to you. But it is more realistic to build connections based on positive behavior, like suggesting that you do some positive things together. Do you think that withdrawing, pouting, and being unavailable will build a relationship?

Accusing

You directly accuse your partner of an indiscretion or of being unfaithful. "Have you been seeing her?" or "Did you have sex with him?" You don't necessarily know for sure what is going on, but you think you need to get your suspicions out in the open. When your partner denies any wrongdoing, you treat this denial as a false pretense—he or she is lying, trying to evade responsibility. You might even try making up accusations, some of which you know are unfounded. But you want to see what kind of response you get from your partner: Does he look guilty? Does she say something that gives her away? You might believe the angry thoughts that come to mind can't be stopped, so you must get them out by speaking them: "I've got to tell you what I really think." You might call your partner a liar, a cheat, a coward for not owning up, and declare that he or she doesn't deserve you. Once you start the accusations, you won't back down. You must prove that you are right. No matter what your partner says, you will keep at it.

Sharon had accused her husband of being interested in other women, of flirting, and even of being unfaithful. Even though she admitted to me that she had no solid evidence—and that her husband seemed to be an honest man—she just felt overwhelmed by her emotions at the time. "Look, I just felt so pissed off I couldn't help myself. I had to say what was on my mind." She was experiencing Emotional Hijacking, and was overwhelmed by thoughts and feelings. So she just let it all out with accusations. Later, when she felt less upset, she reflected on what she had said to her husband: "I feel so embarrassed. He hadn't done anything to deserve this. I just lost control."

The disadvantage of the accusation strategy is that it is likely to drive your partner further away—and drive you further away. You will feel more angry, anxious, and jealous when you start a string of accusations. This is not to say that you shouldn't confront your partner with the facts, if the facts do indicate that something is going on. But if you make a rash accusation, then both of you will remember it for quite some time and it will be hard to recover.

You might think that there are some advantages. Maybe your partner will confess and then you will know for sure. Or, alternatively, maybe your partner will prove that he or she is totally faithful. But how often have you seen the positive side of the accusation strategy? Do relationships improve because of accusations?

Derogating the Competition

When you derogate the person you think you are competing with, you hope to show your partner that he or she is better off with you. You claim that the other person is not as attractive, not as smart, not nearly as successful, as you. He or she is boring, can't be trusted, is dishonest, even disgusting. You may say things like: "She's an idiot, you know that. All she's interested in is advancing her career." "He's always screwing around on his wife. He can't be trusted with my wife." "I can't believe you would find her interesting; she's so boring." "He has lost one job after another." Your rationale is that, if you can convince your partner that the other person is inferior, then he or she won't be interested. And you also hope to find out whether your partner will defend the other person—which you will interpret as a sign that he or she is indeed interested. The more you derogate the other person, the more likely your partner might be to disagree with you, which adds fuel to your suspicions. Any defense of the other person or unwillingness to join your attacks can only mean that your partner prefers the other person to you.

The disadvantage to this strategy is that your partner might start viewing you as irrational, hostile, unfair, or petty—further alienating the two of you. It doesn't build a strong, positive bond. Even if your partner does agree that the other person is undesirable, your derogation can make you sound like a judgmental person who will go on the attack. This is not likely to help your relationship.

You might hope that your partner will see the light, recognizing that the other person is truly undesirable, and that he or she is better off with you. But ask yourself how you would feel if your partner derogated someone you like, through an innocent friendship, or respect, such as a colleague. You might become defensive as well.

Derogating Your Partner

When you decide to derogate your partner, you hope to form such a convincing case for defectiveness and inferiority that he or she feels lucky to have you, and unworthy of attracting anyone else. Your hope is to show your partner that there are no options other than you. You might point out that your partner is a liar, a cheat, an idiot, and ugly. He or she may have declining sexual abilities or be less attractive than ever before. Sharon acknowledged that there were times when she would go after her husband, pointing out his shortcomings, suggesting that he had lost his looks, insisting he was difficult to get along with and ornery a lot, and saying sex wasn't so good. The implication was, why would anyone else want him?

Another way you could derogate your partner is to tell him or her all the terrible things that would happen if you did separate:

"You won't have any money," "I won't let you see the kids," "You will be alone forever." You're cutting off all viable alternatives by convincing him or her of being a loser with no options.

Derogating your partner could also be a punishment for being interested in someone else. By labeling him or her as undesirable, you hope to impart the lesson that, if he or she does anything to provoke your jealousy, then there will be a price to be paid.

The disadvantages of this approach? It will likely drive you and your partner further apart, and it may lead to retaliation—or at least defensiveness. You are not likely to build a strong case that a relationship with you is the desirable alternative. If your partner views you as punitive and hostile, then it could lead to a breakup—not because of a threat from someone else but because your hostility has driven the two of you apart. You are less likely to return to warmth, closeness, and trust. Your hostility can become far more significant to your partner than the positives in the relationship.

You might think derogating your partner will send clear messages: no one can take you for granted and no one can get away with anything. By exercising power and control, you think you will keep your partner, but that might backfire because it is very plausible that he or she could leave you over this hostility.

Threatening to Terminate the Relationship

When your suspicions get more intense, you may test your partner by threatening to end the relationship if his or her behavior doesn't change. You may threaten to leave, throw him out, or never see her again. You may walk out and not contact him—let him worry, let him stew like you have been stewing and suffering. Your ultimatums may sound like this: "If you do this again, I will leave you. You will never see me again." In some cases, you might leave the house to get away from your partner, to threaten him or her with the idea that it all could end.

If you have discovered a real infidelity, it might seem like a sufficient reason to walk out and threaten to end the relationship. But many people are able to rebuild relationships after an affair has been discovered. It's hard, but possible if both partners work on it. It is up to you to decide.

There are some disadvantages to threatening to end the relationship. If you don't follow through on the threat, it may lead your partner to treat your concerns as empty threats—he or she will not take them seriously. You can lose credibility. This may even cause you to feel the need to escalate conflict even further, just to establish the credibility of your concerns. Your threats can also lead your partner to make his or her own threats—your threat to leave might lead your partner to leave. There is high reciprocity for negative behavior, as it tends to lead to negative responses from the other person. Think of a threat to leave the relationship as a last resort. There are many more adaptive, and less risky, strategies that we will discuss later in the book.

You might think there are advantages to threatening to terminate the relationship. By adding to the cost, you may hope to motivate your partner to take your concerns seriously. You may have expressed these concerns many times in calmer ways, but your partner may continue to ignore them. You might believe that you can no longer tolerate your partner's behavior and you would be better off, and suffer less, if you ended the relationship. You may think the only way to handle the intensity of your anger and anxiety is to threaten to leave, which might give you short-term relief. No one can tell you that you should, or should not, terminate a relationship. I tend to think that it is important to consider as many other options as you can. That is, of course, what this book is about. Have you tried all the other options yet?

Increasing the Cost to Your Partner

You may be using threats or punishment to reduce any freedom of movement that your partner might have. You might indicate that, if he or she left you, you would get all the money, you would keep the kids from them, you would ruin their reputation, or you would flaunt your own freedom by having sex with people you both know. You may make it clear that, if he or she continues a current behavior, you might threaten to escalate conflicts, tell family members, withhold sex, or not see them. You might anticipate that their behavior could lead to a breakup—initiated by either of you. With this control option, you have raised the threat level. In some cases, you might end up threatening violence—against your partner, against yourself, or both. You think that increasing the cost will keep him or her attached to you—too frightened to leave, so he or she never will.

What are the disadvantages of this control strategy? As intense and uncomfortable as your emotions might be, trying to control people by threats is seldom a winning strategy in maintaining a relationship. One woman told me that she was so afraid of her partner's jealousy that she would sneak around to see people and was planning to secretly move out of state to escape her husband's threats. It's not possible to control people for very long. While this strategy may give you the sense that you are going to get what you want, it is also likely to alienate your partner even more. He or she may break up with you—not because of another person but because your partner doesn't want to be controlled and threatened by you. Also, this strategy keeps you vigilant and anxious because you are trying to control what is uncontrollable: what someone else thinks, feels, and does.

Some advantages you might perceive include knowing what is going on, keeping things from unraveling, and showing your partner that no one can treat you this way. These concerns make sense in a way, but trying to control someone with threats and punishment may not give you those advantages. Your partner may be more likely to become secretive, withdraw, counterattack, or even leave. The very goals that you want to achieve may be undermined. You cannot control the freedom of another person—and it's not likely that you would want a relationship based on that kind of control. Maybe there is a better way.

Trying to Make Your Partner Jealous

You may try to find out whether your partner is really committed to you by seeing whether he or she becomes jealous when you flirt with, or show an interest in, someone else. You might openly flirt in front of your partner, tell him you are going to see someone else, or let her know that you are thinking about one of your exes. Or you might become secretive and hope that he or she gets jealous, wondering why you are not available or not responding.

If we think our partners are jealous, we tend to conclude that they are committed to the relationship and that they truly care. However, this is a high-risk strategy and can backfire. Your partner might justify his behavior by saying that you are doing the very same thing. Why should you complain about him if you are flirting or seeing other people? Another possibility is that your partner might conclude that she cannot trust you and may then begin to distance herself from you—or even threaten to leave. Your partner may view your behavior as openly manipulative and insulting, then back away—leading to the very thing that you most fear, the end of the relationship.

You might think that this strategy offers an advantage, a test for finding out what kind of relationship your partner is after. If there's no jealousy on display, you might think that he or she doesn't really want a committed relationship. So you might want to reconsider your own commitment. My view is that this strategy is a high-risk one, because people often act in unintentionally destructive ways when they are provoked.

Hedging Your Bets

This is a less-direct strategy in which you look for alternatives to your partner. When one woman was feeling distrustful of her boyfriend, who was often unavailable, she began seeing a married man on the side. Because she was getting needs for sex and communication met by the married man, she felt less of a need to get those things from her boyfriend. As a result, she expressed less jealousy with the boyfriend but felt stuck in limbo between two unappealing alternatives—a boyfriend who had become withdrawn or a married man unable to commit to her. Her self-esteem sank further. Sometimes when people are jealous, they begin revisiting former lovers. They think, "Just in case this current relationship doesn't work, I can probably see that person again." This serves as a hedge, an insurance policy in their minds.

The problem with the hedging strategy is that neither alternative is likely to get better. As you withdraw and become secretive, closeness diminishes with your current partner. You are compartmentalizing yourself, and you may expend a lot of energy hiding your secret life. Another disadvantage is that you may get caught. How would it work out when you have expressed jealousy, but then are exposed as the one who is cheating or hiding things?

The hedging strategy may make you feel less threatened by loss should a breakup occur. It might help boost your self-esteem for the moment, knowing that someone else is interested. It might seem that you have an insurance policy, a fallback position. Those are understandable concerns and it might make you feel like you are more in control for a time. But think about whether you have known anyone who said, "I built a stronger relationship with my partner by hedging my bets." My guess is you haven't.

Is Your Strategy Working?

We have examined some of the more common strategies that you might be using when you feel jealous. Perhaps you use more than one of these strategies, or even some that are not in this chapter. Ask yourself what you hope to accomplish with your strategy, and consider whether it is in your long-term interest.

You might think that you don't have a choice—but you do. By thinking through each of these strategies, you can consider whether it is the only way—let alone the best way—to build respect, trust, and love. Each of these strategies has a rationale that might make sense and, in some cases, might be helpful. We always believe something positive will result from our negative behavior. But each of these strategies has a potential downside, so you need to weigh the risks.

You are not the only one acting on jealous strategies—many people do these things. As you will learn in the following chapters, there are other techniques and strategies that might be more helpful. They also might have less of a downside; after all, who wants a relationship to end because of the strategy used in an attempt to keep it together?

Part III

Turning Jealousy
Around

Chapter 6

Stepping Back to Observe and Accept

Now that you know how your jealous mind operates with emotions that overtake you, and how you cope by interrogating, seeking reassurance, and looking for clues, we are ready to explore some new—more powerful and helpful—ways to live. You will learn how to: step back and observe jealousy without getting hijacked; recognize the difference between thoughts, feelings, and behaviors; and talk back to the negative, overwhelming thoughts that seem so true in the moment. We can make room for jealousy without feeling crowded out by it. It helps to accept that all of us are flawed and imperfect, and that we all have difficulties. With this acceptance, we can live in the real world.

"How Can I Stop Feeling This Way?"

In Jealousy Mode, our thoughts and feelings get stormy. It's like we are caught in a tornado, being tossed around in winds of fear, anger, confusion, and sadness. Thoughts jump at us and take us over. We feel we have no self-control, no ability to get out of the storm. The blaring thoughts and terrifying emotions suck us in, and we often feel there is no chance for escape. Karen said, "I feel like I am possessed by some force beyond my control. When he tells me that he was at a party and ran into his ex-girlfriend, I feel overwhelmed with every horrible emotion that I could ever imagine. I want to scream. What the hell is wrong with me?"

We seem to think our lives should be free of jealousy, anger, anxiety, sadness, and resentments—we should be happy all the time. But life is filled with frustrations and disappointments that can be rough to ride at times. Life is not always going to be the way we want it to be. Sometimes we want *emotional perfectionism*—to be content, at peace, happy, and secure—but life doesn't work that way for us.[34] And it doesn't work that way for anyone. When a painful feeling comes along, we get wrapped up in it—as if it's the only feeling we will ever have. Our emotional perfectionism tells us that things shouldn't be this way.

Because we are hijacked, we think we must get rid of these feelings, banish these thoughts, and clear our minds and hearts. We want peace, clarity, and certainty. Without this tranquility—which seems perpetually beyond our reach—we feel we are lost. But as we struggle more to get rid of these internal experiences, we feel even more helpless and confused. We don't know where to turn. The storm keeps churning inside our heads and our jealous hearts.

Alone and embarrassed, you ask, "How can I stop feeling this way?" You think there is no way to live with these thoughts and feelings. You may even think that in order to stop the storm you need to end the relationship. But you love this person and don't want to lose him or her. After all, isn't keeping your partner what the jealousy has been about from the beginning?

In this chapter, we explore how you can live with thoughts and feelings—even ones that you don't like—without getting hijacked. It's like learning to tolerate the crazy uncle who shows up for a holiday dinner. You stand back, observe, but don't engage. By noticing, observing, and accepting, you can live with the background noise in your head without jeopardizing the relationship that you value.[35]

Making Room for Jealousy

Don't assume the jealousy needs to disappear. Allow it to be there, without taking over. Allow it to be what the two of you can *accept*—for the moment. Allow it to nag you, annoy you, or scare you—without it taking over *everything*. Think of the jealousy as alarms sounding, many of them false alarms. For now, you will recognize that jealousy is here, the alarm is going off, and you and your partner will accept it.

You have heard the sounds before: jealousy is an echo from the street, it is a blaring horn in traffic, it is a shout from an alley. It might pass by. It might wake you up. Allow it to happen without getting hijacked by it. *When you hear the siren on a fire engine go by, you don't need to chase it.*

Imagine your relationship as large enough and rich enough that it can handle and accept the background sounds of a jealous voice. Once you can both accept that it is here, that it sounds off alarms, then together you may be able to take steps toward working with it. It's something for the two of you to learn to live with.

"But," you say, "how can I tolerate these angry and anxious feelings about someone I love? I can't stand having all these feelings. Shouldn't I feel one way?" In the poem "Song of Myself," Walt Whitman describes how he loves the old and the young, the beautiful and the ugly, the rich and the poor. He embraces all of life, all of humanity.

> *Do I contradict myself? Very well, then, I contradict myself,*
> *(I am large—I contain multitudes.)*36

Think of your jealousy as containing multitudes, with a full range of feelings in your relationship. It contains love and hate, peace and conflict, fear and serenity. It is all there, all part of the full experience. We only contradict ourselves when we think we should feel *one way*. Your jealousy is one of the many experiences, ways of feeling, and ways of relating that will be part of this large, complete, human bond.

I'm Not Okay, You're Not Okay— But That's Okay

If you are the object of a partner's jealousy, you are probably demanding—or hoping—that the jealousy goes away and disappears. You want things to be just right with your partner, with peace and happiness. You want it calm and easy.

In 1967, Thomas Harris published the bestselling book, *I'm OK—You're OK*. I guess that he was an optimist. After all, do we really believe that we are all okay? Do we really believe that we don't annoy each other, disappoint each other, and judge ourselves and the people around us? I don't find the book's sentiment to be realistic.

I have a different idea about relationships. See whether it fits your experience: I'm not okay, you're not okay—but that's okay. Because aren't we all a little bit irrational, a little crazy, a little unfair? If you are okay with that, then you can live in this world of imperfect people and fallen angels, and trod through the ups and downs of life. We often wish that we lived in Utopia, a place of perfect harmony. But keep in mind that the word "utopia" was drawn from the Greek word for "no place." You can't get there from here, because it doesn't exist. Here are some ways to view this world, the one we live in, that can help your relationship.

In a Cave Together

Think of it this way. Your partner, who is feeling overwhelmed with jealousy, feels all alone, frightened, helpless, confused. Imagine that he or she is in a dark cave. There are different passageways in this cave. You are there together and you have a small, dim candle. You are trying to find a way out—together.

You are both afraid and feeling lost as you hold the candle. You fear the candle will go out and you will be completely in the dark. But you learn that, if the two of you hold the candle together and breathe compassion into the flame, there is more light. It may be that you don't know which passageway leads to the way out. But you do know that you can walk together.

Love Means Walking Together in the Dark

Just as we need to make room for jealousy in our intimate relationships, we also need to make room for it in our work, family, and friendship relationships. Painful and difficult feelings can arise in any relationship that matters. With your colleagues, you may have an idealized view of how things should be done. Let's say it's that everyone should be fair, all the time. That view would be wonderful if we lived in that kind of world. But we don't. So recognizing that someone else might get more attention than us is a reality we need to be prepared to encounter. We can't continue to say, "I can't believe that happened!" when it seems to be happening everywhere else. Just because things aren't fair does not mean that you can't win the game. We must learn how to live effectively in a world where unfairness is all around us. Successful people know how to get along with unfairness. They don't take it personally and they strategize for success.

Accepting All the Emotions

Making room for jealousy means we recognize that our relationships are complex, so we need to accept a wide range of emotions—not exclusively positive and pleasant ones. We can still love a partner or friend and still have angry, jealous, resentful, and even vengeful feelings toward him or her. That doesn't mean we act on all those feelings, but it does mean that people can frustrate us, disappoint us, annoy us, and let us down.

Our unrealistic desire to have only pure and wonderful feelings toward people in our lives is something I call "pure mind."[37] It's a kind of emotional perfectionism to say, "I should only have positive feelings toward them and they should only have positive feelings toward me." Unfortunately, that's not the real world. The real world is filled with disappointments—along with joy, meaning, and love. But no one is that good. We all are prone to let each other down at some time. The question is: Can we pick ourselves up and repair the damage? Can we survive the empathic failures in which we fail to connect, support, and care in the way the other person expects us to? Living life without disappointment is not a possibility. We all fail at some point, myself included.

We Are All Fallen Angels

What do you do when you are disappointed or disillusioned? Some of us become pessimistic, some build walls around themselves, some attack the world in protest, and some gain realistic and more complex views of life and relationships. I choose the latter.

I have learned that trying to be a saint will have one result: living in hell on earth. Because the truth is that we are all fallen angels. Keep reminding yourself, no one is *that* good. No one is free of jealousy, resentment, envy, boredom, anger, or disappointment. Everyone has a dark side, along with a brighter side—despite our wish that brightness encompass the complete reality. Relationships are not simply about feeling good all the time. Relationships can be difficult, almost impossible at times. It's not always an easy thing to love someone or to be loved. It's not easy having friends, siblings, and colleagues. We can be difficult with each other.

Relationships are about the capacity to feel everything—and to still go on. In place of emotional perfectionism, I would suggest emotional complexity and emotional richness.

Observing Rather Than Struggling

A thought or feeling can become even more powerful when we struggle to eliminate it. We want to shout at ourselves to "Stop thinking the way I'm thinking!" or to scold ourselves for the feelings we have: "You're doing it again, loser, you're feeling jealous." But the more we struggle, the stronger thoughts and feelings become. It's like one of those 1950s atomic-bomb monsters that gets stronger the more we shoot at it with our weapons. It gets larger and takes on the energy of our firepower. When we're busy trying to shoot thoughts and feelings down, the struggle feeds their power. So what can we do when we feel this way?

One approach that is helpful is called "mindfulness," which is simply paying attention to the present moment, without judgment and without trying to control things.[38] Mindfulness allows us to stay here, in this moment, without jumping ahead to the future and without jumping back into the past. It allows us to let go of what we struggle with—thoughts about the past and thoughts about the future—to simply observe the present moment. When we are jealous, we pay too much attention to our thoughts, reliving a past moment and anticipating a future that may never happen. Mindfulness allows us to find a safe space in the present moment where we let go. We can let go by first paying attention to our breath. Let's try it right now.

For a moment, notice your breath. Notice where it is in its cycle. Is it coming in, going out? Just keep your attention on your breath. Don't try to control it, don't judge it—just notice it. Observe your breath in the present moment, notice how it changes, how it flows, how your breath goes in and out. Notice that your mind may drift to other thoughts or sounds, and then gently bring yourself back to your breath. Notice where your breath is in its cycle, notice how it goes in and out.

What if we could do this with our thoughts and feelings? Imagine having the thought, "My partner might be flirting with someone." Imagine that thought is the breath that comes in and out. Imagine watching that thought, as if it is a string of words drifting across the sky. Imagine that you watch that thought slowly moving in a gentle breeze. Imagine that it is moving along with the wind. Stand where you are, and see the thought. Do nothing else, just observe it. It is here and you are watching it. Nothing is happening, the thought is drifting across the sky, you are watching it, standing in the present moment, observing, letting the thought come and go as it drifts along. Notice that you are still here, in the present moment. You are observing your jealous thought and choosing to do nothing but watch it. Another way to imagine this is to see your thought on a movie screen. You are sitting in your chair, comfortable, watching it play out. It is just a movie—one scene and it will pass. You are here, but the thought is over there.

You are not the thought and the thought is not you. You can allow the jealous thought to be on its own. It can drift along, it can call out, but you are safely in your seat. You watch thoughts and feelings going back and forth, noticing how they may pass by. They are on the move. If you don't grab onto the thought, it will drift away. Away from you.

It may also drift back. Watch it, let it come and go. Like your breath, like the waves on the shore, gently coming and going. You are here. You are watching. You are making room. You are letting things be.

Mindfulness of the Breath Exercise: In this exercise, you simply sit and observe your breath—without judging how you are doing, without trying to control what you are doing. You simply observe and let your breath come and go. The purpose is to practice observing the present moment and letting it go with six simple instructions.

1.   Find a comfortable, quiet place to sit with your back straight.

2. Focus your attention on your breath and notice it going in and out.

3. Simply observe your breath as it gently flows back and forth.

4. Notice that your mind goes elsewhere—to thoughts, memories, sounds.

5. Gently bring your attention back to your breath.

6. What do you notice about your mind?

   • Is it wandering to other thoughts and sounds?

   • Is your mind busy a lot?

   • Are you chasing after your mind rather than staying in the present moment?

   • Are you judging how you are doing?

You may find that your jealous mind hijacks you and that you get carried away when these thoughts and feelings pop up. With some mindfulness practice, you can imagine that these jealous thoughts and feelings are simply outside sounds. You can observe them and then bring your attention back to your breath or to the present moment. You can observe the jealous thoughts, and then let them go for the moment.

Validating Your Jealousy

You may have been struggling with jealousy for some time—perhaps in other relationships, often secretly as you keep these thoughts and feelings to yourself. You may feel confused or ashamed, thinking there is something terribly wrong with you. Your jealousy may spring on you at any moment—when your partner is away, you two are socializing with other people, you are alone and think about his or her former lover. It seems that it can come at any time.

It is hard for you. Your jealousy is not something that you wished for, it is not something that you planned. At times, you think that no one really knows how hard it is for you, and you can't confide in the one person you are closest to—your partner—the object of your jealousy. Because whenever you tell them about your feelings, it seems to backfire. You partner may say:

- Leave me alone.

- This is your problem.

- I didn't do anything wrong.

- You must be insecure.

- Why are you so neurotic?

And this only makes you feel worse. So I am going to suggest a different way to look at your jealousy—I am going to suggest that you have a right to all of your feelings. We don't tell someone with a headache to "Just get over it." We don't tell someone with indigestion, "There's no reason to feel this way." These are your feelings. Your anxiety, your sadness, your anger, your jealousy. These are yours for the moment.

For now, stand back and respect the feelings for what they are: a part of your experience at the present moment. A difficult part—but this is your experience. Allow yourself the right to have your feelings.

Now, this doesn't mean that your thoughts about what is going on are based on facts. They may be, or they may not be. But facts are different from feelings. I can feel sad because I believe I will be alone forever, but the sadness is true for me simply because I am having that feeling. But I might be wrong about the future—about being alone forever. We won't know until we find out what the facts are. But our feelings are indisputable. And sometimes they are difficult in the moment we feel them, so we need to validate our feelings. Validation is acknowledging the truth. And the truth is that you are having jealous feelings, they are your feelings, and they are painful.

Validating Yourself Exercise: You can validate your jealousy by saying to yourself:

- These are my feelings right now and I have a right to feel what I feel.

- These are difficult feelings for me and I need to accept that difficulty.

- It is hard to have these feelings when you care about someone, so this is hard for me.

- Sometimes I will feel alone and unable to express these feelings—which makes it hard.

- I am not alone—jealousy is part of human existence.

We often think that jealousy is only a sign of a problem. But you wouldn't feel jealous if the relationship meant nothing. So I also recognize that jealousy may come from positive values and the commitment that you have to someone. Jealousy is your recognition that someone is important to you, that commitment, honesty, depth, and love mean so much to you. Ask yourself whether your jealousy is the painful sign of love and commitment. Respect yourself for having values of love, intimacy, romance, and loyalty. After all, your jealousy shows how connected you are. And it reflects your fear of losing that connection. Let's look at my conversation with a client who was struggling with jealousy.

Bob: Sometimes jealousy is related to the positive values that we have, like the value of monogamy, commitment, honesty, closeness. Are these values that you have?

Carol: Yes, of course.

Bob: So, one way of looking at your jealousy is that things matter to you. You are not a superficial person when it comes to a relationship. You take things seriously.

Carol: Of course I do.

Bob: What if your partner said to you, "You know, I think everyone should be free to do what they want to do, so if you want to go out with other people—and have sex with them—that would be okay with me." If your partner said that, what would you think?

Carol: I would think that he wants to screw around with other people. I wouldn't trust him.

Bob: In a sense, you would want your partner to be capable of jealousy, because it would be a sign of commitment and a sign that you matter to him.

Carol: Yes, if he wasn't jealous, I would think he couldn't be trusted. I would also think that I didn't really matter to him.

Bob: Perhaps jealousy, just like any emotion, has a positive side and a negative side. I think it's important to recognize that jealousy not only makes sense, but may be a capacity of commitment and trust.

Carol: That makes me feel a lot better about who I am.

The first step in validating your jealousy is to recognize that these are your painful and difficult feelings. The next step is to see your worries, anger, and anxiety as coming from the fact that *someone matters to you.* You are jealous because someone you value, a relationship you value, may be threatened. It's essential to affirm the importance of love and commitment, the values of intimacy and honesty, the desires for depth and meaning. Yes, those are important. But, at times tragically, the anger and anxiety of jealousy are the result. You feel things because things matter to you.

So you are locked in what seems like a dilemma—loving someone, but fearing them too. How difficult this must be. Validate the difficulty, the dilemma, and the conflict within you. Make room for what is inside you. You are filled with multitudes.

Another way to validate your jealousy is to recognize how universal an emotion it is. As discussed in chapter 1, we can find jealousy throughout the world, in different cultures, in different historical periods. We find jealousy in children, even infants. In animals, even insects. So understanding the universal nature of your feelings may help you feel less alone, less uniquely upset. When we recognize that our feelings and needs may be universal, we can accept them. We can allow them to be for the moment.

Consider the way you are seeing things. If you believe that your partner might betray you, we can understand how jealous feelings would arise from that belief. We can see that a lot of people might feel jealous if they believed that their partners might betray them. If you think, at times, that you would have a hard time living your life, or that you would feel humiliated, if your partner betrayed you—then we can understand how strong your emotions might be. Whether you find out that your perceptions are right, wrong, or in a shade of gray, these are your perceptions at the present moment and they may overwhelm you with painful feelings. Validating your feelings means also recognizing that your thoughts and perceptions may be linked to those feelings.

If you have a history of betrayal—if past lovers have cheated on you or if your current partner has been unfaithful—it's understandable that you would feel jealous. This would make you prone to having these feelings, and to seeing a possibility of betrayal in your current experience. If one or both of your parents was unfaithful, or left, or wasn't there, we can also understand that you might feel anxious. Because this would set the groundwork for difficulties with trust, and make you more sensitive. So, yes, understand that what you are experiencing right now may include past experiences as part of it.

And we should validate that it may be possible that your partner is not completely trustworthy. Maybe there is something to your suspicion, maybe your partner is not completely transparent, maybe he or she is not as reliable as you would prefer. Maybe you are right, at times, that there is something going on. So you may be responding to suspicions that could be shown valid. But even so, even if your thoughts and feelings make sense, even if there might be something going on, there is still a lot that we can do to help you cope.

It's important to validate the feelings you are having, to respect your own feelings. Own them as yours, recognize that sometimes feelings are painful, it feels painful to love someone, we get hurt, and people let us down. Sometimes our fears come true. Yes, recognize that, validate it, and understand how it feels and why it hurts. And know that, even when we accept and validate what we feel, it is also possible to cope better.

Stepping Back from Jealousy

Validating feelings doesn't mean getting hijacked by them. You can acknowledge your anxiety and anger in the present moment, you can point to your jealousy and say, "I can see that I am feeling that way again," but you stand back, stand apart, and take a moment to reflect. As you step away from the feelings for a moment, ask the following questions.

- Do I really want to get hijacked by these thoughts and feelings?

- Do I want to feed my jealousy? Or do I want to step back from it?

- What will happen if I let this take over?

- What will happen if I act on the feeling?

- Is it possible that I might be misinterpreting things?

- What are some things that I can do to cope better, in the present moment?

When we step back like this, we can see biases, thoughts, actions, and responses with more clarity. While validating the pain, we can also examine the thoughts that contribute to the pain, how we may act on our jealousy, and how we respond to our emotions—while still acknowledging them as painful. Having those feelings is hard enough, at times, but interrogating, scolding, punishing, threatening, following, ruminating, and worrying only add to our pain. Thoughts and feelings don't have to dictate what we do or what we say. We can find other ways of coping, better ways. We are not slaves to our minds. We decide. We step back, think, and consider the options.

See whether there is a different way of coping with the way you feel. For example, you might learn that—while the way you feel at present might seem overwhelming, everlasting, and out of control—your current emotions are temporary, not necessarily destructive, and they don't need to control you. Think about what can put things in perspective to help you stand back, accept, observe, solve problems, build a bigger life, engage meaningfully, improve communication with your partner, and learn that this life you are living is not dependent on any one person—except yourself.

Having Compassion for Yourself

No one knows how hard jealousy is for you like you do. No matter how understanding, how empathetic, or how caring your friends or partner might be, no one is going through the experience right now like you are going through it. Your jealousy comes from a fear of being betrayed or abandoned by someone you love. It may be the most difficult set of emotions that you have ever had. There are times when you might be angry at yourself for having these feelings, times when you feel embarrassed that you are feeling the way you feel, and times when you fear that your world is collapsing in front of you.

This is a time to stand back from the present experience of overwhelming feelings and to think about yourself as someone you care about, someone you respect, someone you love. We can call this *compassion*, because you want an end to your suffering and pain, you want to direct caring and accepting love toward yourself. You want to embrace yourself—along with your jealous heart—by imagining wrapping your arms around yourself, holding yourself, and assuring yourself that you will always try to be on your side. This is how you can care and soothe the broken heart within.[39]

You are always with you. You can always love you. You need the love, so why not give it to yourself? Why not always be on your side?

You can imagine the most compassionate, warm, loving person from your childhood or among your friends saying to you, "I love you, I care about you, I accept you." Imagine this person wrapping his or her arms around you, holding you gently in a soft and loving embrace, being completely here with you at this moment.

Imagine that you are loved—*by you*. And imagine that you are always with yourself, always there to hold yourself in your heart. When you fear the loss of love, remind yourself that you are always here to love you. Then you can feel peace for the moment, as a serenity that blankets you, a calm that envelops you. Even in a storm, it can be calm in this loving embrace.

Now that you have taken a step back, to observe, listen, and allow jealousy to be there, you can start to examine your thoughts.

Chapter 7

Living with Your Thoughts

When you have a jealousy thought, have you ever tried yelling at yourself to snap out of it? "Stop!" you might say, "Enough!" If you've done this, has it worked? In psychology, this is known as *thought stopping,* and psychologists used to even give people rubber bands to put around their wrists. When they had an unwanted thought, they would snap the rubber band against their skin to literally try and "snap out of it." But the idea behind thought stopping implies that thoughts are to be feared and must be avoided. The problem is that unwanted thoughts keep coming back—*they rebound.* No one can be snapping all day and all night. And it can even convince people that they can't live with unwanted thoughts—that they must get rid of them.

If you are doing something similar with jealous thoughts, you'll find that you need to pay attention to the thoughts to suppress them. You look for more jealousy thoughts and—*presto*—you will find them. But what if you were looking for something completely different? What if you were looking for the clouds in the sky, the sound of rain on the roof, the colors of the books around you, or were trying to notice your breathing as it goes in and out? You can acknowledge and accept the jealousy thoughts, but shift your attention to something outside of you—something else. Notice what you are focusing on, and ask yourself if there is something else that might be more important, more relaxing, more peaceful.

In this chapter, we will go over ways to live with unwanted thoughts so we can get on with our valued behavior—regardless of the background noise that seems to bombard our minds.[40] We don't have to chase the ambulance we hear in the street, we don't have to listen to the conversation at the next table, and we don't have to take every telemarketing call we get.

In the same way, rather than snap at yourself when you have a thought, you can use a wide variety of powerful techniques to live with the noise. Just because a thought appears in your mind doesn't mean that you need to spend the whole day with it. You have a choice. You can acknowledge it, say to yourself, "I see that thought right there," and then get on with other things. It's like noticing a small mailbox on the side of the road as you drive past. You don't stay and rummage through it. The same approach works with jealousy thoughts—you can notice them, point to them in your mind, saying, "There it is again," but then keep going with what you are doing. Allowing them to simply *be* allows you to live with them for now—without being controlled by them.

How Neutral Thoughts Become Major Life Events

During the course of any day, you experience thousands of thoughts and images. But at the end of the day, you are likely to forget almost all of them. Pause your reading for a minute, close your eyes, and try to recall what is immediately around you, wherever you are sitting.

I am sitting in my study. With my eyes closed, I can imagine the monitor to my right, a window in front of me opening to a cloudy sky, a pile of files in a basket on the floor, a chair stacked with books, and a cat at the door hoping to come help me write. But honestly, except for the cat, I really didn't notice these things when I first started writing this chapter. I was focused on the thoughts in my head, the words on the screen, and my urge to check email again. In other words, there are a lot of thoughts, images, and sensations floating in and out of our temporary awareness, but—unless we pause to really pay attention—we will forget about them.

Certain kinds of thoughts appear in our immediate awareness that we give more attention than others. Some of these thoughts may be pleasurable, like the thought of talking to my friend and his wife at dinner tonight. But other thoughts may be disturbing, like jealous thoughts. If you are prone to jealousy, you may have a lot of these disturbing thoughts: thoughts about your partner flirting with someone, thoughts about your partner's former lover, or thoughts about your partner cheating on you. When these thoughts appear in your awareness, you quickly become concerned. It's as if your mind says, "Put everything else aside and *pay attention to these thoughts!*"

These are known as *intrusive thoughts*, because when they occur in your mind, you have a sense that they are unwanted and negative. You activate your strategy about jealous thoughts. What is the strategy? It's a series of steps your mind takes that turn a rather neutral occurrence of a thought in your mind into a major life event. Here's what you think about your intrusive thoughts:

1. "That thought is important"

2. "I need to pay attention to that kind of thought"

3. "That thought stands out—it means that something is going on"

4. "If I have that thought, it means my partner can't be trusted"

5. "That thought can help me predict what will happen"

6. "That thought can help prevent me from being surprised"

7. "I have a responsibility, to myself, to check things out and find out what is really happening"

Let's look at each step in this sequence. Starting with the thousands of thoughts and images you have throughout the day, you are suddenly treating certain thoughts as more important than other thoughts. A jealousy thought becomes quite important—its simple occurrence is important to you. You don't brush it aside. You don't say, "That's silly" or "That's just a thought," like you do with other thoughts. Instead you say, "That's important." Because it's important, you then feel you need to pay attention to thoughts like this. So you begin focusing on any occurrence of a jealousy thought and, of course, you find what you are looking for.

The reason you find jealousy thoughts is that you are asking yourself, "Do I have any jealousy thoughts?" Simply asking the question means that you must have a jealousy thought. So your mind sets out, looking for jealousy thoughts that you find over and over. Other thoughts are overlooked, discarded, ignored. You are on a search—*a thought hunt*—in your anxious mind. And you find what you are looking for—more jealousy!

Now that you are looking for jealousy thoughts in your mind—and finding them over and over—you conclude that the occurrence of the thought means something real is going on. The thought is not some random thought; it's not just noise in your head. You see it as a warning signal, an alarm, that is telling you something. And at this point, you begin to think that simply having the thought means your partner cannot be trusted: "It's possible that my partner could be looking around—I just had that thought—and so maybe she is. Maybe I can't trust her." You are treating the thought as *evidence for distrust*. It's like being charged with a crime and the prosecutor says, "Someone had a thought that you are a criminal. That's the evidence." And the judge pounds the gavel and bellows from the bench, "Guilty as charged."

So you begin treating these thoughts as self-protection. They are helping you, warning you of a possible betrayal, alerting you to the possibility of things unraveling. This operates just like an early distance warning system: the thoughts are going to help you see the missiles being launched, before they strike. These thoughts are your protection—with them, you won't be surprised, you won't be hurt, you won't be humiliated. So you don't want to let your guard down; you don't want to turn off your alarm system.

All these alarm thoughts are sounding, and now you must find out what is really going on. Is there a fire? Is your partner lying? Is something happening? You don't say, "Oh, that's just a thought; I can ignore it." No. At this point, you say, "That's a thought I have to do something about." So you begin looking for evidence—and it's a biased search. You are looking for clues to confirm the thought: small signs that your partner is losing interest, that she is flirting, that others are interested in her. You even look into your *imagination* for evidence: "If I can simply imagine it, then it must be true." So any fantasy or image that you form of your partner talking, flirting, or touching someone becomes evidence of guilt.

Evaluating Intrusive Thoughts

You have evaluated your intrusive jealousy thoughts, and you find them to be immediately important, personally relevant, and predictors of what is going to happen. But let's pause a moment and think this through; let's think about your thinking. Maybe the evaluations are misleading. Maybe there is another way to look at these thoughts. Maybe you don't have to get stuck on them, be hijacked by them, let them mislead you, and then go down the rabbit hole of jealousy.

Let's evaluate your evaluations of jealous thoughts. Look at them again, and then compare them with another way of looking at things. You have been treating the simple occurrence of your jealous thought as an important event. What if the thought is *simply a thought?*

1. "That Thought Is Important"

Not necessarily. Maybe the thought is simply a random firing in your brain. Maybe it's an old habit of thinking. Simply having a thought does not make the thought important. It's only a thought.

2. "I Need to Pay Attention to That Kind of Thought"

You don't need to give a lot of attention to a thought simply because it occurs. You can simply notice it and then let it go. You don't have to dwell on it. You have thousands of thoughts every day that you don't dwell on. Letting go of certain thoughts might help you get on with your life.

3. "That Thought Stands Out—It Means That Something Is Going On"

You have had these jealousy thoughts countless times and many have been false alarms. A thought is not a barometer; it's not a temperature gauge. It's only a thought. Thoughts are not always connected to what is going on.

4. "If I Have That Thought, It Means My Partner Can't Be Trusted"

Whether your partner is cheating or not, it is not based on your having a thought—it's based on his or her behavior. You can examine the evidence later, but it makes no sense to conclude that you can't trust someone simply based on a thought. Imagine a court of law—would simply having a suspicious thought be sufficient evidence of anything?

5. "That Thought Can Help Me Predict What Will Happen"

You can ask yourself how many times you had suspicious or jealous thoughts and have been wrong. Predicting reality is not based on a thought—it's based on testing out predictions. Can you find any evidence that you have been wrong in the past with your predictions?

6. "That Thought Can Help Prevent Me from Being Surprised"

Continually predicting betrayal does not help you, even if your partner were to betray you. You would be upset no matter what. But focusing on your jealous thoughts will only make you feel angry, sad, and anxious—keeping you miserable. If you ever were betrayed, you would be upset with or without these thoughts.

7. "I Have a Responsibility, to Myself, to Check Things Out and Find Out What Is Really Happening"

If there is overwhelming evidence that something bad is happening—yes, you should check it out. But simply having a negative thought doesn't mean you need to turn into a detective. It only adds to your misery and will lead to more conflicts in your relationship.

Here is a clear way to contrast problematic and helpful ways to think about jealousy thoughts.

Problematic Jealousy Thought: "My partner could cheat on me"	Helpful Jealousy Thought: "My partner could cheat on me"
"I must pay attention to that thought"	"I can accept the thought and get on with my life"
"That thought is very important to me"	"That's background noise"
"I have to do something now"	"I don't need to take action"
"I need to find an answer"	"The thought is like a telemarketing call; I don't need to pay attention to it"
"There must be some reason why I am thinking this"	"That's just a thought"
"If I have that thought, something is going on"	"I can make room for lots of thoughts"

Do I Need to Hang Out with Jealous Thoughts?

We have thousands of thoughts and images that come to mind every day. Most of them are fleeting images and ideas that pass by like the wind, so we have stopped noticing them. But when it comes to jealousy thoughts—"My partner might lose interest and go off with her" or "I wonder if she found her ex-boyfriend to be sexier than me"—we get stuck on them. We spend a lot of time hanging out with these thoughts, engaged with them, entangled in them, and we can even feel trapped by them.

Daniel felt that jealousy took over his mind. He couldn't get away from these thoughts, he felt stuck, as if someone had started a conversation with him on an airplane. He couldn't just get up and leave, and the flight went on for hours.

So let's look at how you can cope with spending a lot of time focused on these thoughts, worried and ruminating.

Productive Versus Unproductive Thoughts

I make a distinction between productive worry and unproductive worry. For example, a productive worry is something that I can take action on today—it's on my to-do list. If I can do something today that will substantially advance toward a solution to this problem, then it is productive worry. For example, a productive worry might be, "Do I have a flight reservation for my trip?" I can check this in five minutes and answer that question. If I don't have the reservation, I can make it today. That's my to-do list for today. It's productive because *there is something to do.*

An unproductive worry might be, "When I give my talk, will people find it boring?" There is not much that I can do today to solve that problem. No matter how much preparation I do, I can't guarantee that people will find my talk interesting. So the thought is unproductive.

Ask yourself whether your jealousy thoughts are productive or unproductive. If you have the thought that your partner might be flirting with someone at work, is there really anything that you can do today to solve that problem? If not, it's unproductive.

What's the problem with unproductive jealousy worries? Simple. Ask yourself how you feel when you engage in endless worries about your partner. Do you feel anxious, sad, angry, helpless? That's the cost of spending a lot of time dwelling on this stuff. It just makes you miserable. Because dwelling on these thoughts will not lead to productive action, you are wasting your time and doing something that will only make you miserable.

Once you realize this, what can you do? You can start with *accepting those thoughts*. But how do you do that?

Accepting Your Jealousy Thoughts

You may have noticed that when you have a jealousy thought, you set off running after evidence, asking questions, and looking for clues. It's as if the jealousy thought appears as an unwelcome guest and starts ordering you around. "Go find out!" "What is really going on?" "Who is he talking to?" "Does she still find me interesting and attractive?" You don't just accept the thought and let it be. No, it's something you engage in, try to figure out, and obey.

One way you can get around this is to think about your jealousy thought as a visitor. You can imagine that you are at a holiday dinner. You notice that, at every holiday dinner, there is an eccentric aunt or uncle who shows up. Maybe her views on politics are a little extreme for you, or maybe he goes on for too long talking about a trip to the shore. And you simply feel bored because, if you are smart, you have learned that arguing with him or her is pointless. You have now learned, after many holiday dinners, to simply compartmentalize and think, "Well, that's Uncle Jay going on again. I guess I will just sit here and listen." I suggest turning yourself into an *observer* of Uncle Jay, and just watch him go on, accepting it for now. His banter is not relevant to you and what he says is not important. After all, it's just words.

So think of jealousy thoughts as visitors—guests—who show up, talk a lot, but what they say is not important. Accept these thoughts for the moment. Let them have their say. Recognize that they are harmless. Let them bounce around as you sit back, observe, and simply let them be.

Ken was at a party and his girlfriend was talking with a handsome young man who seemed very friendly. Ken noticed he had some jealousy thoughts. "Maybe she finds him attractive" and "I think he is flirting with her." He decided to stand back and accept these thoughts—to recognize that these were natural thoughts to have when his attractive girlfriend was talking with someone. He just accepted the thoughts and decided not to do anything. He didn't go over to talk with her and interrupt her conversation. He just accepted his jealousy by thinking, "I guess I am having some jealousy thoughts right now." He then went over to some friends of his and started talking, allowing the jealousy thoughts to lurk around, hang around, have their say. And he decided to do absolutely nothing. Later, he felt less anxious as a result.

What If Jealousy Thoughts Are Just Thoughts?

I said earlier that jealousy has a *mind of its own*. It has a pattern of core beliefs about other people and about us, a rule-book about how people should act and feel in a relationship with us, and a set of thinking biases—like mindreading, personalizing, and fortune-telling—that can take us down a dark path of anger, anxiety, and desperation. But a thought occurrence does not mean that we need to be hijacked. After all, isn't a thought just a thought? Are thoughts real? It's true that we are really having a thought. But the thought may not reflect the reality outside of our heads. Here are three helpful ways to recognize the nature of a thought.

Is a Thought Real?

Close your eyes. Imagine the face of a dog—any dog. It can be a golden retriever or a poodle. Any dog face will do. Get a clear picture in your mind of that dog's face. Watch it carefully. Once you have that picture in your mind, hold it for two minutes.

Then open your eyes. How did you feel when you had your eyes closed? Did the dog's face remind you of anything? Did you feel anything? Was it a dog you know—or once knew? When I did this exercise just now, I had an image of our dog Jane. She was a wonderful dog. I felt sad because she died three years ago. We loved her. My feelings were real. Even so, when I opened my eyes, Jane was not here.

Simply having a thought or an image may feel real, making us feel anxious, sad, happy, relaxed. But it doesn't always point to something that is real, existing, and happening outside of our heads. The same thing occurs when we have jealous thoughts. The thoughts pop into our minds, "Maybe he is flirting with someone," and we treat that thought as important, as signifying that something is happening or will happen. It's as if the thought and reality become one: I have the thought, therefore the reality must be there. This is *thought-action fusion.*

But they are not one and the same. When I opened my eyes, my dog Jane wasn't sitting here. So what is a thought?

Thoughts Can Be Like Telemarketing Calls

Have you been unfortunate, like me, and picked up your phone only to hear the voice of someone trying to take a poll or sell you something? This is not someone you know; it is a company you've never heard of. It's a telemarketing call.[41] I find these calls annoying, but they are going to keep happening.

What do you say when telemarketers call? Do you feel an obligation to talk with them? You might, if you are very polite, but maybe you just don't have the time or interest. I say, "Take my name off your call list" and hang up.

You can view your intrusive jealousy thoughts as telemarketing calls. You can think, "Oh, it's that telemarketing call about jealousy. I can just let it ring. I don't have to answer that. The caller will eventually give up. I have better things to do." Just because something is ringing in your head doesn't mean you have to pick it up. Let it ring.

Thoughts Can Be Like Trains in the Station

Another helpful way to think of thoughts is to imagine them as trains in the railroad terminal, coming and going.[42] You are looking for the one train heading for Peacetown. All the other trains you may see in a given moment are going elsewhere: Anxietyville, Distrust Town, and Anger City. Yes, they kind of look like the train to Peacetown, but they're headed other places. So if you board the wrong train, you will get lost and have a hell of a time trying to get back. So watch carefully, because hopping on a jealousy thought can be like getting on the wrong train. Observe it, look at it, and choose not to get onto it.

I find it fascinating to watch train cars going by. I like to imagine where they might be going, what the journey is like for the conductor, and what the passengers are seeing as they pass through the countryside. Your jealousy thoughts can be on that train as it goes by. Who knows where they are going? The train is passing you by, on a long journey. You decide not to get on that train. The whistle blows and it disappears over the horizon. You simply decided that this particular train can continue on without you.

Setting Aside Jealousy Time

You may have mixed feeling about jealousy thoughts.[43] On the one hand, you believe that these thoughts might be helpful—you might find out what is happening, they might warn you, they might protect you. Maybe you won't be surprised. But you also may believe that these jealousy thoughts are out of control, that you can't concentrate on anything else, and that you need to get rid of them completely. So you have both positive and negative views of your jealousy thoughts: "I need them to protect me and I have to get rid of them." In your efforts to get rid of them, you might tell yourself, "Stop thinking this way," but then the thoughts just bounce back—at times, they return even stronger. This worries you because you think, "If I can't suppress them completely, then I will not be able to cope with them—they will take over."

One technique for coping with jealousy is to set up jealousy time. You can set up an appointment with your jealousy at a specific time every day. It's an appointment that you put into your calendar. Rather than spending a lot of time with jealousy thoughts in the morning, afternoon, evening, and even in the middle of the night, you can set aside twenty minutes each day for them. For example, at 3 p.m. each day, you will spend time dealing with these thoughts. And if the thoughts pop up at any other time, you can say to yourself, "I will put that off until 3 p.m." You can write them on a piece of paper or save them in your smartphone. That way, you won't forget these thoughts. You will have them at 3 p.m. Many people assume that they will be unable to delay thinking about these thoughts. "I have no control," they say. But in most cases, we are able to put them off until later. What happens when you set aside jealousy time?

- You learn that you don't have to obey a jealousy thought and respond to it right at that moment. You are free for a while.

- When jealousy time rolls around, you might realize that you are having the same thought over and over. So there is no reason to repeat it over and over in the future—you got the thought, okay, now you can move on.

- You may find that when jealousy time finally comes around, the thought doesn't bother you as much. This is important to notice, because when the power of a thought dissipates on its own, you can see that thoughts don't have to be so important to you when you have them. Thoughts and emotions *change over time*—often a very short period of time.

So what can you do during this jealousy time? Here's a simple tool that you can use when you are bothered by recurrent jealousy thoughts. You can use this at any time, but it's especially helpful during an assigned jealousy time.

Becoming Bored with Your Thoughts

Have you noticed that you eventually lose interest in things that once bothered you? Maybe you have lost interest in, or forgotten, that a former boss said something unpleasant to you or the fact that someone didn't invite you to a dinner party. At one time, you were really upset—you felt angry, you vented, and you thought it was close to the end of the world. But now the topic is boring to you. You reached a state of *benign indifference*—you just didn't care anymore.

Imagine we showed you a favorite movie 500 times. Maybe you enjoyed it on the second or third showing—maybe you saw something new both times. But after a while, you got bored. You couldn't pay attention. Even the thought of seeing it again makes you uneasy. You think it will be hard to sit through again, you're so bored. You even fall asleep. The dialogue becomes empty. Nothing holds your attention. Even the popcorn tastes bland.

I've been using this technique for years, and I call it *the boredom technique*.[44] It's simple to do.

1. Take any one of your jealousy thoughts. Let's say the thought is, "My wife could end up cheating on me."

2. Repeat that thought very slowly 500 times, for about fifteen minutes. The first twenty-five times you say it to

yourself, your anxiety may go up—more than it has before. Stay with it.

3. Don't get distracted, just keep your mind on the words.

4. Repeat the thought very, very slowly—almost like a zombie on sleep medication: "My wife could end up cheating on me."

5. Try to focus on each word: "My wife" or "My husband" or "cheating." You can even draw out the word so that every letter is intoned.

6. You can do this silently if you wish.

7. If you are like almost all my clients, you will find that the thought becomes boring eventually. You just can't keep your mind on it. This is what I call *the boredom breakthrough*.

It's a simple technique, based on a very fundamental principle in psychology called *habituation*. Habituation simply means that repeated exposure to a stimulus, like your thought, decreases how much it will elicit a response from you. It's also called *flooding* because you are flooding yourself with the feared stimulus. If you have a fear of being on elevators, I would ask you to ride with me on the elevator twenty-five times. The first few times you might feel very afraid—maybe even terrified. After ten times, your fear has dissipated. After twenty times, you are bored. Even if your fear doesn't subside, in the future your fear will decrease. Thus, simply being willing to face your fear—being willing to do what feels hard to do, over and over—leads to less fear in the future.

How does this work with jealousy thoughts? Each time you had a jealousy thought, you felt the need to do something about it: to find out what is happening, to worry about the future until you had absolute certainty, or to get reassurance. Now that you have the boredom technique, you are intentionally practicing having your feared thought without trying to do something about it. You are not neutralizing the thought by getting information. You are not trying to take control. You are welcoming the thought in, practicing it, repeating it, until you find yourself bored.

> Ken practiced the boredom technique every day, once in the morning and once at night, for fifteen minutes. As he repeated the thought for the first few minutes, he was more anxious, but after a while his anxiety decreased. After two months of using a lot of the techniques in this book, I asked him which one was the most helpful. He said, "By far, it is the boredom technique. I know I can do it, I know that the thought will bother me less, and I know I don't have to be afraid of the thought. I don't have to really do anything—except repeat some words."

Listening to Thoughts as Background Noise

We all have an ability to automatically ignore background noise, because if we paid attention to every little thing, we would not be able to function. When you are in a restaurant with your partner, if you simultaneously noticed every single sound in the restaurant—the waiter banging around dishes, people walking across the floor, the music in the background, multiple conversations among twenty nearby people, the sound of a fork being placed on a table, the sound of your own eating—you would probably feel you are going insane. So our minds have a *gating system* that filters out irrelevant noise, keeps us focused on what we want to focus on, and prevents us from getting distracted.

Some people have difficulty with distraction, as their attention gets captured by extraneous sounds, sights, and smells. And it may be that you are getting distracted by your jealousy thoughts because you decided that they are very important. You decided you need to pay attention, that they warn of danger, and that if you ignore them you will end up bewildered, betrayed, and devastated. But during most of the day, you are not having these thoughts—especially when you are asleep. Your guard is down, you are not focused on your jealousy, you are letting things go for a while. Why hasn't the world fallen apart during those times?

When you have another jealousy thought, you might find it helpful to say to yourself: "That's background noise. That's not something I need to pay attention to." And let it go. Try this experiment to get more of a sense for background noise.

1. Stop reading for a moment and close your eyes.

2. Listen to what is around you.

3. What sounds do you notice? Maybe you notice the air conditioning or the air circulation. The sound of your own breathing. The traffic outside. Or footsteps in another room.

4. Try to notice sounds that you otherwise don't notice. These sounds are always there—but you treat them as background noise.

5. You accept those sounds, you let them happen, you don't get stuck on them. You just let them come and go. They pass by, whether a whisper or a police siren that is five streets away, so that they are barely noticeable.

What if you were to treat your jealousy thoughts as background noise? Just another sound, another breeze, another passing moment that comes and is gone in an instant. Another insignificant, unimportant moment. Another forgettable experience. You are not trying to get rid of the jealousy thoughts. You are not trying to stop them. You are just putting them into the background.

In the foreground of your attention, you can focus on positive goals—and you can keep the jealousy thoughts in the background. Focusing on positive goals is important, so every day, have a set of positive goals for yourself. This could be exercising, eating healthful foods, being rewarding and supportive to your partner, playing with your children, completing a work project on time. Positive goals can represent your values and advance your life as you want to live it.

Making Room for Jealousy Thoughts

You have been plagued by jealousy thoughts, feeling that you can never escape them. They intrude on your mind, take over your consciousness, and seem to be the lens through which you see daily life. You've tried to tell yourself to stop having these thoughts, you've told yourself that you've got to get over this, but nothing seems to work. They are still there. You ask a friend, someone you trust and respect, "How can I stop thinking this way?" and your friend tries to comfort you and says, "Just tell yourself to stop." That makes you more depressed and anxious because you've tried that hundreds of times and it never seems to work for more than a few minutes.

Let's try something different. Let's make room for your jealousy thoughts. Imagine that your mind is an enormous room, constantly changing, getting larger or smaller day by day depending on what you focus on and what you do. Now imagine that your jealousy thoughts are in this large room, a room where you will make space for these thoughts.

Think of these thoughts as something you can put in a jar. Put that jar up on a shelf. Once in a while you take it down, spin it around, look at it, open it up, take a taste, think about it for a few minutes, and then put the jar back up on the shelf. The jar is always there; you are keeping the jar. But there are lots of things in the room, lots of things outside the room. The jealousy jar is only one object, one thing. It's there for now.

Like the cans and jars in your pantry that have been sitting there for years, there is an expiration date. You don't know what the expiration date on your jealousy jar is, but I can tell you that at some point *you simply won't care.* At some point you will think, "I guess I can throw this out." At some point, it might disappear on its own.

Turn the Tables: What If Your Partner Were Jealous of You?

A powerful technique is to imagine that your partner is jealous of you. This *turn the tables technique* encourages you to imagine what it would be like if he or she looked at all your behaviors from a suspicious perspective.

> Jacob was jealous, thinking his wife might be flirting with someone. He was worried that she was developing an infatuation with her boss. He was focusing on her behavior—primarily what he didn't know about her behavior when she was out of sight at work. He imagined the possibility that she could come up with the same reasons to be jealous of him. We tried a role-play, in which I pretended to be his wife accusing him of flirting, wanting other women, having past sexual relationships. This led Jacob to realize that anyone can build a case. And he ended up laughing at the jealousy.

If your partner could build a case for feeling jealous about you—and you know that you are not up to anything—then it might help you realize that anyone could be a target of jealousy. Anyone can be suspected and we never really know for sure what is going on.

Keep in mind that simply having a jealousy thought, or even feeling angry and anxious, doesn't mean that anything is really going on. We can notice our thoughts, stand back, observe them, treat them like background noise, recognize that—like the noise from the street—they will come and go, and focus on productive actions that move things forward. We often get hijacked into thinking that our thoughts need to be answered, that we must obey our thoughts, that there must be some really good reason we are having our thoughts right now. But we are bombarded by thousands of thoughts and images every day. So it's important to know what will make our lives better—and being hijacked is not the answer. Sometimes the answer is to simply not respond to the worrisome questions of our negative thoughts.

Chapter 8

Talking Back to Your Jealousy

For every thought, there is another way of thinking. A key element of cognitive-behavioral therapy—as I discussed in part 1—is to look at our thinking habits and examine the content to see whether we have biases or predispositions and then to consider alternative ways to view things.[45] With jealousy, we may have *mixed motives*—we may want to feel less jealous, but we may be reluctant to look at things in a different way.

In chapter 4, we looked at how jealousy can be magnified by a set of biases in your thinking. This is your tendency to see things in ways that may confirm your suspicions or jealous thoughts. In this chapter, we will use a lot of powerful techniques to help you see things more realistically. Understand that when I say "biases," I don't mean to say that your perceptions are always wrong. You could be right in your jealous thoughts—maybe your partner is lying or planning on being unfaithful. But let's assume, for a moment, that you don't know for sure. All you know is that you frequently have jealous thoughts, you are upset, and your thinking may have jumped to the wrong conclusions in the past.

In this chapter, we will look at how your automatic negative thoughts and other biases can trigger Emotional Hijacking. These include:

- Mindreading: "She is interested in him"

- Fortunetelling: "He will cheat on me"

- Personalizing: "She's yawning because she finds me boring"

- Labeling: "He's a cheat"

- Discounting the positives: "Her affection for me doesn't really mean anything"

Each of these thoughts can be examined using the facts and logic we will explore in this chapter. We will also examine whether your rule-books and assumptions are helping or hurting you. These are thoughts that say things like these statements:

- "If someone flirts, you can never trust them"

- "We should always have great sex because without it, my partner will look elsewhere"

- "When I don't know for sure what is happening, then it means my relationship is in danger"

If it turns out that statements like these are hurting you, we will explore ways to replace them with guidelines that make your life easier to live. We'll also dig into core beliefs about yourself and other people, which might include the following beliefs:

- "I am unlovable"

- "I am helpless without a partner"

- "I am basically defective"

- "Men can't be trusted"

- "Other people will reject me"

- "Other people will demand perfection from me"

We will review ways to reverse many of these core beliefs to become more realistic, less negative, and more self-affirming. You can call on a number of simple and powerful techniques to defeat them. With this chapter, you will be fully armed against your jealousy.

Questioning an Automatic Negative Thought

Let's start with automatic thoughts. For many of the automatic thoughts we have, we can ask a series of questions that may give us alternative ways to view things. You are considering developing a new habit of thinking: *there is another way to look at things.* So let's take the thought "My partner is flirting" and apply some of these techniques.

We'll assume that there is some room for doubt. I know that there are times where there can be no doubt. But for the sake of this exercise, assume that it's possible I don't know for sure. The thought, "My partner is flirting" is an example of mindreading because I think that I know what's in the mind of somebody else—I think I know what his or her intention or desire is. Here is a series of questions to pose, and I'll give examples of some possible answers.

What Is the Cost of Thinking This Way?

The cost of thinking that my partner is flirting is that this makes me anxious and angry, adds to my jealousy, and I might do things or say things that I will regret later.

What Is the Benefit of Thinking My Partner Is Flirting?

Maybe I can catch things before they get out of hand. Maybe I can detect a threat that's real and protect myself from the threat.

When examining the costs and benefits of a jealous thought, there is no implication that a thought is false. You are only looking at the consequence of thinking this way. For each automatic thought you have, ask, "If I were less likely to think this way, how would I feel and what would my relationship be like?" Consider whether there is any way that you might be better off in the long term if you were to think this far less frequently and less intensely.

What Is the Evidence in Favor of This Thought?

My partner is smiling while talking to somebody else. I am interpreting smiling and talking as evidence that she is flirting.

Is There Any Evidence That She Is Not Flirting?

My partner is friendly, smiling, and interested in talking to other people—including people of the same gender and people who I know my partner is not sexually attracted to.

When you look at the evidence, you might ask yourself: What is the quality of the evidence? Is this evidence open to a different interpretation? For example, could it be that your partner is simply a friendly person?

How Would Someone Else Interpret This?

If other people see my partner smiling and talking to someone else, they might not immediately conclude that she is flirting. It may be that someone else, who is not emotionally involved, might have a very different interpretation of my partner's behavior. They might think she is friendly, polite, or charming.

If It Were True That My Partner Is Flirting with Someone Else, What Would That Mean to Me?

I might have a string of thoughts: "If my partner is flirting with someone else, that means she doesn't respect me"; "He cannot be trusted"; "She will cheat on me." Looking at the implications of the thought is important because these implications may be connected to fundamental, basic fears—such as fears of betrayal, abandonment, or an inability to be happy without my partner.

Considering Alternatives to Automatic Thoughts

Let's look at a few typical, negative, automatic thoughts that you might have that may feed your jealousy, and see whether there might be alternative ways of looking at things. Keep in mind that we are examining and testing out your thoughts to see whether there is a different way of looking at things. This is not meant to invalidate your thoughts or feelings. But if your thoughts don't stand up to examination—and if they are making you upset—you might want to consider the possibility that there is another way to look at things.

Mindreading

This is interpreting the thoughts, feelings, or intentions of another person, as with the thought, "My partner is interested in somebody else." The fact is, we generally don't know what other people are thinking—because their thoughts are private. Do you think your partner always knows what you're thinking? No. If you engage in mindreading, you may be feeding a lot of jealousy with ideas that may or may not be valid. Consider the costs to you and to your relationship. Mindreading probably makes you more anxious and angry, you focus painfully on other people interacting with your partner, and this may increase the likelihood of arguments with him or her. Some alternative ways of thinking about your mindreading include:

- Mindreading often upsets me so, if I do less of it, I might feel better

- I don't know what my partner is thinking

- Maybe my partner is thinking of something else entirely—work, me, the news

- My partner could have the same attitude about me and wonder if I am interested in someone else

Fortunetelling

This involves your tendency to project what will happen in the future without sufficient information. For example, you might predict that your partner may be unfaithful to you, will leave you, or is planning a rendezvous with someone else. Engaging in fortunetelling on a regular basis adds to your worry, makes it difficult to live in the present moment, leads you to ignore the positives that you might have in your life, and may cause more conflicts with your partner. Consider the following questions, which point to alternative ways to respond to your fortunetelling.

- What is the cost of thinking this way? Is it making you anxious, angry, and jealous?

- Is there any advantage in engaging in this, on a regular basis?

- Does fortunetelling really make you safer? Or does it make you feel less safe?

- Does this lead you to interrogate and try to control your partner?

- You may, or may not, be right about the future. But can you feel that consistently engaging in negative fortunetelling only adds stress to your daily life?

- How many times, in the past, have you been wrong about what you thought was going to happen?

- What is the evidence that your partner is going to act this way?

- What could be the reasons why he or she would not act this way?

Personalizing

This is when you take things very personally because you believe that your partner's behavior is directed against you or reflects something about you. For example, your partner seems less interested in intimacy tonight. As a result, you conclude that your partner no longer finds you attractive and is interested in somebody else. It's easy for us to take almost anything personally. I've even noticed that some people take it personally when the elevator is slow or they are stuck in traffic. The problem with taking things personally in your relationship is that you're going to feel threatened daily. Consider alternative interpretations of what's going on. For example, if your partner seems to be less interested in intimacy, you might consider the possibility that he or she is tired, has something else in mind, is distracted by a challenge or problem, or is feeling less desire due to an argument that you were having with each other earlier. Here are some additional ways of responding to your tendency to take things personally:

- There is no advantage to continually taking things personally

- It only adds to anxiety, anger, and jealousy

- Not everything that your partner does is related to feelings or thoughts about you

- Not everything that you do is related to your partner

- Maybe your partner has something else on his or her mind

- Your partner's friendliness with someone else may just be friendliness and nothing else

- Your partner is with you because he or she has positive feelings about you; otherwise, he or she wouldn't be with you

Discounting the Positives

Sometimes we ignore or discount positive things that are happening in our lives and focus on the negatives. For example, you might focus on the fact that your partner is talking to an attractive person while you ignore the many demonstrations of affection that your partner has been giving you all evening. When you discount the positives in your relationship, you may lose sight of the strong bonds that hold the two of you together. You may unintentionally stop rewarding him or her for positive behavior—which can cause your partner to feel taken for granted. Your partner may become demoralized and conclude that there is no sense in engaging in those positives. Another consequence is that you will become demoralized and focus on the negatives found in your biased perception.

An alternative to discounting or ignoring the positives is to try refocusing from the negatives to the positives. Tell your partner about the positives when you experience them: "I appreciate that you took the time to talk with me about my work" or "I appreciate that you are helping out with the chores." For two weeks, try to catch your partner *doing something positive*. These positives can be very simple behaviors such as talking to you, complementing you, helping out, spending time together, or many other things. Every day, keep a written record of the positives that your partner engages in. This will help you notice that there *are* positives in your relationship and may offset your bias.

You may object and say, "Why should I have to focus on those positives? Shouldn't my partner do those things anyway?" Yes, it may be true that you expect your partner to do positive things in a relationship. But even if you were to assume this, it will be very helpful for you to *notice* them—because that is what relationships require. A complaint I hear frequently from couples having difficulties: both partners believe that they are not appreciated, they are taken for granted.

Are there times when you feel taken for granted? How would you feel if your partner began noticing your positives and complimented you daily? I suggest experimenting for two weeks. Catch your partner doing good things and see whether you feel any better. When we notice positive behaviors and reinforce them by complimenting people, those positive behaviors increase in frequency. The things we reward others for doing tend to occur more often. Here are some challenges to your tendency to discount the positives:

- What are the costs of ignoring the positives in the relationship? If you take things for granted, your partner may not feel appreciated.

- Will focusing on the negatives lead you to strengthen the positive bond that the two of you share? Probably not.

- Make a list of positives that your partner has directed toward you in the past.

- Make a list every day to keep track of, and count, your partner's positive behavior.

Labeling

This occurs when you give a general description of your partner, or a type of person, recognizing neither the variability nor shades of gray in yourself and others. For example, you may label your partner as "neurotic," "manipulative," "pathetic," or "a liar." You make a general statement as if it can capture the entire person your partner is. The problem with a general label is that you end up ignoring any positive behaviors as you focus on a few negative behaviors.

Ask yourself how you feel when somebody labels you. It's as if your entire existence is limited to this label. You have been reduced, canceled out, and there is no room for change. It's likely that, when you label your partner, he or she will become defensive and it will escalate into arguments.

An alternative to labeling is to describe your observation as a single behavior that you would like changed. Then describe what the change would look like. For example, instead of labeling your partner "a liar," you might say to him, "I would feel better if you could tell me, honestly, who you spent time talking to at that meeting." To help you step away from labeling your partner, you might consider all the behaviors that are inconsistent with a negative label. If you label your partner as being "manipulative," you might consider all of her behaviors that are not manipulative. People are complex; their behavior varies across various situations and with different people. Recognizing this complexity and variability will give you a more realistic and adaptive way of coping with your jealousy. Here are some questions to consider as you look at your tendency to label.

- What are the costs of labeling? Does it make you angry, anxious, jealous, hopeless?

- How do you feel when someone labels you?

- Are you missing some information when you label your partner?

- What is some evidence that your partner engages in behaviors that are not consistent with this label?

- In a given situation, could there be factors that might account for your partner's behavior? For example, your partner runs into an ex-lover and is genuinely happy to see him. Could she simply be happy to see someone she once liked?

- Rather than label your partner, can you identify some specific thoughts, experiences, or factors in the situation that might lead him or her to act in a certain way?

- How can you encourage your partner to engage in positive behaviors that you both might enjoy?

Exploring Rational Responses to Automatic Thoughts

Here are more examples of common automatic thought biases, with suggestions for alternative ways of thinking about each one. See whether any of these might be helpful to you.

"She thinks that our relationship is over, so she is falling for her boss."

Mindreading: You assume that you know what your partner and others are thinking without having sufficient evidence that these are their thoughts.

Rational Response: "This is probably not true because she is talking about ways we can be happier together. She wants to take vacations together. She does love me, which is why what I say to her hurts her so much."

"He will run off with someone else. We will break up and get divorced."

Fortunetelling: You predict the future negatively, that things will get worse or there is danger ahead.

Rational Response: "There is no reason to think this. We have had arguments before and we get over them. We have been together many years and, when we are not arguing, we have a good time. We love each other."

"It's awful that we have these arguments. It would be even worse if she betrayed me."

Catastrophizing: You believe that what has happened, or could happen, will be so awful and unbearable that you won't be able to stand it.

Rational Response: "The arguments are unpleasant, but when we step back and put them in perspective, we realize all the good things that we have. We don't need to define our relationship as one big argument."

"We have a terrible relationship because he is a total liar."

Labeling: You assign global, negative traits to yourself, others, and your relationships.

Rational Response: "We have a human relationship, with some good things and some bad things. The good things are that we respect and love each other, and we try to be supportive of each other during difficult times. We can have fun together and we will continue to."

"Just because she says she loves me doesn't mean she won't cheat on me."

Discounting Positives: You claim that the positive things about you, or your relationship, are trivial compared to the negative things.

Rational Response: "We have a lot of good things together. We find each other interesting, we have good times together, we enjoy a lot of the same activities, we enjoy talking."

"Look at all the negatives in our relationship: arguments, depression, anger, anxiety. So much seems bad that he's probably looking for someone else."

Negative Filtering: You focus almost exclusively on the negatives in your relationship, and seldom notice the positives.

Rational Response: "There are some negatives, but I can also see many positives. Just looking at the negatives is depressing and unrealistic. Let me keep track of the positives."

"Another argument. These arguments go on and on."

Overgeneralizing: You perceive a global pattern of negatives on the basis of a single incident.

Rational Response: "That is not true; we can go a week without an argument—sometimes longer. We need to change the style that we have when we argue. We used to listen to each other, accept that there are different points of view, and try to problem-solve together. If there is a pattern, it is that we stay together and work things out."

"We are constantly arguing because she flirts with other men all the time."

All-or-Nothing Thinking: You view events or people in all-or-nothing terms: it is either all good or all bad.

Rational Response: "No, we argue once or twice a week, and then it escalates. Most of the time we have a good time together. I need to look at the variations between good things and problems that arise rather than viewing our relationship as just one way or another."

"We shouldn't have so many arguments. We should be excited and turned on by each other all the time, because then I'd feel more secure."

Shoulds: You interpret events in terms of how things should be, rather than simply focusing on what is.

Rational Response: "Well, it would be nice if we were perfect. We aren't, so we can work at deescalating the arguments we have. And relationships aren't perfect, either, so I guess I can understand that sometimes my partner isn't in the mood for intimacy when I am."

"If she finds another man interesting, then it means I must be boring."

Personalizing: You take things personally in your relationship, as if anything that your partner or others do reflects on you.

Rational Response: "There are a lot of people who may be interesting at times and I don't have to be interesting all the time. If she finds someone interesting to talk to, it doesn't mean anything about how she feels about me."

"It's all his fault that I'm jealous. He is making me jealous by talking to her."

Blaming: You focus on the other person as the source of your negative feelings, and you refuse to take responsibility for changing yourself.

Rational Response: "No, we both share the blame and we both can change the way we respond. I know that my response to him talking to another woman is up to me."

"I feel anxious, so that means my partner is up to something."

Emotional Reasoning: You let your feelings guide your interpretation of reality.

Rational Response: "Feeling anxious doesn't mean that he is seeing someone else; it means that today is a rough day for me. By this evening things can get better and they usually do."

Examining the Underlying Assumptions in Rule-Books

We have just looked at your automatic thoughts that contribute to your insecurity, anger, and jealousy. But these negative, automatic thoughts that you have can be fueled by underlying beliefs. As I described in chapter 4, these underlying assumptions are known as rule-books. You can recognize them because they are often "If...then..." statements. "*If* my partner finds someone else attractive, *then* it means he doesn't want me and he can't be trusted." Imagine if you didn't have that rule-book, and you simply thought, "We all find other people attractive because other people are attractive. It doesn't mean anything about his desire for me and it doesn't mean that I will be betrayed."

Rule-books arise automatically, almost without any reflection. They often include beliefs about the way things *should be*: "My partner should only pay attention to me" or "My partner should tell me everything that she is thinking and feeling." We can ask many of the same questions about our assumptions as we do about our negative, automatic thinking.

Look at the Costs and Benefits of a Rule-Book

Let's look at the costs and benefits of believing that "If my partner is flirting, then she cannot be trusted." The cost might be jealousy, anger, taking things personally, and even retaliating against your partner or against other people. You might think that there's a benefit to this rule—that you can keep your partner from being friendly with other people by criticizing him, trying to make her feel guilty, or even threatening to leave the relationship.

Ask Whether the Rule-Book Is Realistic

One way of assessing your rule-book is to ask whether it fits the real world. In other words:

- Is it realistic to think that your partner will never find anyone else attractive?

- Is it realistic that your partner will never be friendly with anybody other than you?

- Is it realistic that you would be the only person that he or she has ever enjoyed having sex with?

You may think that your life would be better if your partner never found anyone else attractive. But the world may not be set up to meet your ideal standards. So you may find yourself continually frustrated by living in the real world.

Apply the Rule-Book to Yourself

Another way of testing your assumptions is to ask whether you could apply this rule-book to yourself. Is it also true that: you should never find anyone else attractive; you have never enjoyed sex with anyone as much as your partner; you never flirt with, or act friendly toward, anyone other than your partner? And if you did flirt, then is it true that you cannot be trusted? When you have a hard time applying this standard to yourself, then you might have a double standard. Do you think you would pass the test?

Explore How Your Rule-Book May Be Perceived Differently

It can be helpful to have standards that are more *flexible* or *realistic*. The thought that "My partner is flirting with somebody" might bother me because I conclude she does not respect me. But let's take that belief and examine it. If someone is flirting, does that necessarily mean lack of respect for me—or could it mean other things? My partner might flirt because somebody is flirting with her, and her response might be natural, almost a reflex. In other words, she may not be thinking about disrespecting me. It's not her intention to hurt me.

Another reason why she might flirt is that it's a habit of hers that precedes our relationship. She may simply be flirtatious and charming—which was one of the reasons that I found her attractive in the first place. She could also flirt because it boosts her self-esteem. Flirting may be a habit that gives her affirmation from other people. To overcome my belief that she doesn't respect me, I can look for other evidence that she does respect me. Perhaps she shows that she cares about me by making spending time with me a priority in her life.

Examine How Your Jealousy Beliefs Reflect Something Negative About You

Sometimes we interpret our partner's behavior as a reflection of something about us. Let's take the rather frightening thought that your partner could cheat on you. Many of my clients not only worry about their partners cheating, but they are also quite concerned about what the cheating would *mean about themselves*. For example, Walter believed: "If my wife cheated on me, then it would prove that I'm a sucker, that I am inferior to other men, and that other women would reject me because I'm a loser."

Let's think about this as we take Walter's thought "I am a sucker if my partner cheats on me" and see whether it really makes sense. If someone steals something from behind your back, does this make you a sucker or does this mean that the person is a thief? In the same way, if your partner cheated on you, doesn't that say more about your partner and his or her character? Isn't it more about *them* and less about *you*? If your partner lies or cheats, it doesn't really mean anything about you. Rather, it means that your partner has failed to live up to the promises that he or she has made. Ask yourself: What would you think about another man whose wife cheated? In most cases, you would think that the wife had failed to keep her promise of fidelity. You would probably think less of her for doing it. Let's look at my conversation with Walter.

Bob:	How would your wife cheating on you make you inferior to other men?
Walter:	Well, it means I wasn't able to hold her interest. I wasn't good enough for her.
Bob:	In what way would you not be good enough for her, if she were to cheat?
Walter:	Maybe I'm not attractive enough for her.
Bob:	But you've been married for eleven years. You told me that your sex life is quite good and that she wants to have sex with you. How is that consistent with the idea that she doesn't find you attractive?
Walter:	Yeah, I know, she always seems to want to have sex with me. I know. But if she cheated, it would mean that she has lost interest in me.
Bob:	Let's look at what we know so far. We don't have any evidence that your wife is cheating on you. We also

know that she wants to have sex with you and that she's been with you for eleven years. If she were to cheat on you, wouldn't it say something about her and her own reasons rather than some specific failure on your part?

Walter: I guess she has low self-esteem, which I knew when we were dating. I don't know. Maybe if she did cheat it might be about that. And maybe that's one of the reasons why she flirts sometimes.

Bob: So the idea that "If she were to cheat, then it would mean that Walter is a failure" doesn't seem to hold up to facts or logic. Fearing that someone will cheat is a very fundamental fear that would bother almost anyone if it were to happen. But what we're looking at here is your belief that it would mean that you are inferior to other men.

Walter: Yeah, I know, it doesn't seem logical. But I guess I also worry that if we were to break up, I would not be able to find anybody else.

Bob: I can see why that would bother you because you value having a committed, intimate relationship. Let me ask you, what would your best friend say about your best qualities?

Walter: My best friend is Merv. I've known him since high school and we're really close. I think he would say I'm a very loyal friend, I'm generous, I'm caring, and I am intelligent. And he would say that I have a good sense of humor and I'm a fun person to be around. I think he believes that I'm a good father to my son and a good husband. Though he knows I'm not perfect. Yeah, he likes me.

Bob: Are there other people who have a very positive view of you?

Walter: Yeah, almost everyone I work with really likes me. And I have a lot of friends whom I've known for a long time. People tend to like me.

Bob: Does that sound like the kind of person whom other women might be interested in meeting?

Walter: I guess it does. But I've been married such a long time, I've never thought of cheating.

Bob: And could we consider that being married a long time also means you're very capable of having a long-term relationship? Would that be something other women would be looking for, in the unlikely case that you were not married?

Walter: I haven't been a perfect husband.

Bob: The very fact that you can recognize you're not a perfect husband might also be a strength of yours. You're not arrogant. Maybe that would be attractive to someone. What do you think?

You can look at your underlying fears, like Walter did. Because of his beliefs about what her cheating would mean about him, Walter became very concerned when his wife flirted. It was a signal to him that she might be unfaithful, which would mean that he is a loser, unattractive, and that nobody else could want him.

Keep in mind that the idea of a possible betrayal can be upsetting to almost anyone. But for each person, betrayal by a partner has unique implications. Look at what these implications are, because they may be making you terrified, distrustful, and jealous. Here are some possible implications of betrayal. Read the following list and ask yourself whether any of these have a hold on you. *If my partner betrayed me, then...*

- I am a sucker

- I am unattractive

- I am a lousy lover

- Other people will look at me as a loser

- This proves I can't maintain a relationship

- I have failed

- I would never be able to find another partner

- All my future relationships will fail

- I cannot be happy on my own

- I could not survive on my own

Sometimes the core fear is so overwhelming that it drives much of our jealousy in the present moment. Consider the possibility that your present relationship is not completely essential to your happiness or your well-being. I'm not saying that your present relationship is meaningless or that your relationship is going to end. No, I'm simply asking you to consider the possibility that you could *survive* and maybe even *thrive* if the relationship did end.

"What If I Am Betrayed?"

What would life be like if you were betrayed? This may be your fundamental fear that is beneath your jealousy. Often people who believe that they have no alternative to a present relationship are much more likely to be jealous.[46] In other words, if you think that the only source of satisfaction you'll ever have in a relationship is the present one, you are far more likely to be anxious about losing it. However, if you believe that you might have other alternatives in the future, you may be less jealous in your current relationship. And when you are less jealous and less desperate in your current relationship, then you might have a better relationship. So look at the idea that you could be happy outside of this relationship. Consider that you could find meaning and fulfillment elsewhere.

Kathy feared that she would be miserable forever, alone forever, if her husband cheated on her. She had been married for eight years and had a son with her husband. Her fear was that if her husband cheated on her, she would never be happy again. Here is my conversation with her.

Bob: Let's keep in mind that we don't have any evidence that he is cheating on you. But we need to be realistic that anything could happen. So we'll follow that line of your fear and see whether there's an alternative way of looking at things. You said that you can't imagine ever being happy again if you and your husband were to break up. Before you met your husband, what sort of things did you like doing?

Kathy: I enjoyed my work, I had a lot of friends, I enjoyed school, sports, travel, reading, and just living my life.

Bob: It sounds like there were a lot of things that you enjoyed doing before you met your husband.

Kathy: Yes, I guess that's true.

Bob: Okay, are there things that you have enjoyed doing in the last eight years that did not involve your husband?

Kathy: Actually, pretty much everything I described to you I have enjoyed doing without him. I like seeing my friends, and I also understand that he's not all that crazy about some of my friends. So a lot of times I see my friends on my own. I take yoga classes, which is terrific for me because I can just relax and stretch. I have some friends I've met through that. And I enjoy my work. I'm doing fairly well in my work and people respect me there.

Bob: So you enjoyed a lot of things in your life before you met him, and many of those things you still enjoy even though he's not around when you do them. Would it make sense that you would enjoy some things in your life, even if your relationship ended?

Kathy: I guess that's true. I do have a lot of good things going on in my life.

Bob: If you did break up, and I'm not saying you will, would there be new opportunities or new things that you might do?

Kathy: Yeah, I guess so. For one thing, I would be dating other men, I guess, although it's hard to imagine that after being married for eight years. And I might go back to school and get a master's degree, which is something I've always wanted to do. Come to think of it, there are places where I would like travel that my husband doesn't want to go to. So I guess I would travel to those places. Yeah, there would be new things to do, new people. I don't know for sure, but I guess there would be a life for me.

Bob: It's natural to think that a breakup would leave you devastated forever. But I was just wondering whether you have ever gone through a breakup before.

Kathy: Yes, I had a breakup in college. And three years before I met my husband, I went through a breakup with someone I had been involved with for two years. I've been through that before.

Bob: And when you went through those breakups, did you also think you would never be happy again?

Kathy: Yes. In fact, I remember even wanting to kill myself at one point after a breakup because I thought I would be unhappy forever.

Bob: I can see that breakups are scary for you. They seem to trigger the idea that you would be alone forever and that you would be depressed forever. But it turns out, given your history, that you eventually do okay after the initial difficulty of breaking up. Eventually things get better. We should keep that in mind.

Kathy: I guess that's true when I look back to the past. But it doesn't seem to be true at the moment.

Bob: Even so, we should keep that in mind that you believe you'll be unhappy forever, but then that turns out not to be the case. If you had known that you would eventually be happy, even without a relationship, do you think you would have been as miserable after those breakups?

Kathy: No. If I believed that, or if I knew I'd be happy again, I would not have felt so devastated.

Bob: So those previous relationships were not essential to being happy in the future, were they?

Kathy: No, they were not essential.

"Can I Trust Anyone?"

You might have the fear that, if your partner were to betray you, then you would never be able to trust anyone else again. So let's think about that common conclusion when there is a betrayal.

Again, I'll remind you that I am not in any way concluding that your partner is untrustworthy. But let's imagine that he or she betrayed your trust. What does this mean about trusting other people?

After a betrayal and after a breakup, it's common for the partner who was betrayed to tell me, "I'll never trust anyone in a relationship again." This immediate response may be a protective strategy we use to keep ourselves from being hurt immediately after a betrayal, especially when we are recovering from the relationship. It might be a good idea to take things very slowly after a breakup, if one were to occur.

Let's look at the logic: If you were betrayed by one person, then you would never trust another person again. Can that one example be generalized to the entire universe of people? Is this realistic? It's like concluding that, if someone stole something from me, then everybody is a thief. That doesn't seem logical and it certainly doesn't seem helpful. Let's imagine that you are out dating again after a breakup. You meet someone you really like and she tells you that her partner had cheated on her, so she cannot trust you. She has concluded that nobody can be trusted—*ever*. Would that make sense?

Never trusting anyone again would be a very hard way to live your life. And you may know some people who went through breakups, who were betrayed, and who did not trust again. This overprotective strategy only limits people from finding new relationships, new happiness, new meaning.

You might also know people who were betrayed and later formed good relationships with new people. These are people who might have viewed the betrayal as a reflection of the person who betrayed them—without generalizing it for the entire population. Trust is something that comes and goes, and it may feel like it has completely been eliminated. But then later, it comes back. In fact, you may have already experienced this after other breakups. Life goes on.

Look for Survivors

Another way of looking at your worst fears is to see whether other people you know have survived a betrayal. Are there people you know whose partners cheated on them and they were still able to lead good lives? Most people know someone who went through a breakup resulting from betrayal. Do you? Maybe the person you are thinking of doesn't have a new relationship at the present moment, but does that mean he or she is miserable every moment of the day? Probably not. It's very likely that, even if they're not in a new relationship, their lives have ups and downs.

People tend to be *resilient*, and they tend to bounce back from losses—even from betrayal. People have gone through your worst fear: they have been betrayed. But they have continued with their lives and, in some cases, have found even better relationships afterward. This can give you reason to believe that surviving betrayal is a possibility. Because when you believe that your life could turn out as good as the lives of people who have survived your worst fear, then perhaps you might be less worried, maybe even less jealous, in your current relationship.

Chapter 9

Putting Jealousy in Context

In chapter 7, I asked you to think about your mind as a large room, filled with different objects, filled with memories. Imagine now that your relationship is also a vast room. It is not simply this one thing—jealousy—not simply one feeling. Imagine richness, complexity, many textures, and all kinds of pictures. All these are part of this relationship.

The Relationship Room

Your relationship room is a space—a mental space—with a kaleidoscope of memories, feelings, thoughts, experiences, disappointments, hopes, and sensations. Looking at it is like looking around the room you are sitting in. I am in my study, which is filled with piles of books, lamps, papers, pens, a couple of chairs. I see one book, in particular, that brings back memories, thoughts, ideas, feelings. I see another book that I know I want to read, but I haven't gotten around to it yet. This is the room, surrounding me with objects, images, memories, and possibilities. There is not simply one thing in it, one feeling, one experience, one moment in time. It extends into the past and into the future. In the same way, your relationship room holds the many experiences that you share with each other. Some may lie forgotten, under layers of memories, until they surface at unexpected moments. Whatever you are experiencing in this relationship room—including your jealousy or your partner's jealousy—it is only one moment, one layer, one possibility.

Imagine your relationship with your partner as a room. Perhaps it is in disarray, like my study. To find something that you want, you need to search around. Perhaps it is filled with reminders, images from the past. It is also filled with the range of feelings you have experienced over these past months, maybe over these past years. You have been spending a lot of time with those feelings of jealousy, anger, anxiety, and sadness. They are here and they have been troubling you. But this room is vast: in addition to the present, there is also the past and the future, as this room goes back and forth in time.

You look around this large, complex, seemingly ever-changing room that includes so many things you may have forgotten—until this moment. You remember when you first met, your first date, even what you wore. How you felt back at the beginning. You remember the walks together, the laughter, the questions that each of you wanted the other to answer. You remember the first time you made love, what it felt like—and the many times after. In this large room, hidden under whatever hides things in your room, you discover—once again—the feelings that you had when you felt so close, so safe, so happy. You think, "Whatever happened to that?" as if it is gone forever. But here it is, in your room. Here it is, in front of you, in your mind, in the feeling of this moment.

As you look around the room, your mind travels back into the past and you remember the fun, the laughter, the playfulness. You remember longing to see each other, missing your partner when apart, wanting to hold her, to be held by him. Yes, you remember how it felt to share something special—maybe it was dinner at the restaurant you both loved or walks you took together, things that might seem ordinary to someone else. But it was you being together, it was something that you felt belonged to the two of you, together. As your mind drifts to those memories at this moment in time, right now, you feel the warmth. You feel the love that you feared was being lost, and you feel sadness because you still fear losing it. Because it was once the two of you.

What was it about your partner that so moved you? That made you feel, "Yes, this is the one"? It is hard to put your finger on it, hard to find the words. And that is what you search for right now: the words. Behind words, there are waves of emotions and images and memories, each seeming different from the one before, some seeming like they will cancel out the others, but they keep coming, one after the other, coming toward you, through you, memories of the two of you. Your memories, your waves of feelings. Your contradictions. Because in this room that both keeps changing and remains the same, your room, you realize that life is filled with contradictions. Where there is hope and love, there can also be sadness and anger. The waves may knock you down, both of you may fall, but you can still struggle to stand, still rise above hard times. If you can imagine holding the hand that reaches out, or reaching out yourself, you can lift yourself above these disappointments. You don't know, you don't want to get your hopes up, because both of you have been knocked down.

Spin Your Relationship Lens

Perhaps your jealousy is like a lens that darkens everything you see about your relationship. Through it, you see your partner and yourself. It seems stuck on the one thing that makes you feel trapped, hopeless, unloved, and unloving. You can only see your partner through one lens, one darkened and dim shadow of reality. There is nothing else, you think, and the emotions of anger and anxiety and sadness you feel at this moment seem inescapable. There is no way out.

I remember looking into a kaleidoscope for the first time when I was a kid. I felt like I had entered an entirely new world. I turned the wheel and the patterns changed, I spun it around backward and the patterns changed again. All I could see was that the patterns were symmetrical and that, each time I moved the wheel, another pattern would emerge. I have often thought that relationships are like kaleidoscopes: each time I turn the wheel, I see a new pattern. I know that, when I am angry, I get stuck on a very dark pattern—one that seems to capture everything—but just leaves me in the dark. In the moment of my anger, it's a pattern I see as I think, "This is the way it is." And it bothers me. I feel trapped by this darkness, this disappointing pattern, this dead end. Then I wonder: What will happen if I spin the kaleidoscope? What if I change to a different pattern? What will I see? What will it feel like?

Let's try spinning the wheel. Let's see what other feeling patterns can emerge when you look at things differently. When I spin a wheel, I am going to call up a different emotion. For now, it will be a more neutral relationship than your partner. Give it a try.

Compassion Lens

Try the emotion of compassion. Imagine, from your memory of childhood, someone who seemed to have compassion, who seemed to hold you in loving-kindness. What do you remember about him or her? For me, I recall my grandmother, who smiled and spoke in a gentle voice, who held me and told me how wonderful I am. Call up memories of this person, bring them into the present moment. Close your eyes and remember being held, touched, comforted. Imagine that feeling of compassion and kindness surrounding you, enveloping you. Here, in the midst of love, you feel safe.

Now imagine feeling love and kindness toward this person. Yes, you feel it right back as you say to yourself—to him or her—"I love your gentleness, I love your kindness, I love you." You feel love flowing from your heart to his or her heart. One heart together. One.

Playfulness Lens

Now I want you to recall another emotion, just for the present moment. Think of a memory when you were playing, laughing. Remember that moment. For me, it is a memory of walking our dog in the woods, along a trail. I was watching her running and sniffing. As I remember, she is playing in my mind, in my heart, in the present moment. I am playing with her. I take a tiny football and throw it for her, watching her chase it. Her tail is in the air, her mouth is open and breathing while she runs. I see her grab the football and bring it back. With this memory, I feel a rush of happiness, a rush of playfulness.

Lenses with Many Emotions

As I think of the good times with my grandmother and my dog, I also feel a rush of sadness because they are no longer with us. But I know what that compassion and playfulness felt like with them. And I know I can still feel those things at times; they never left me completely. I can feel them now, even in memory, even with the sadness. Yes, *both feelings* came. The compassion and the sadness, the playfulness and the sadness. Sad that they are gone, but happy with the memories of being hugged, of watching my dog running for the ball.

That's the nature of feelings and memories in the relationship room. Feelings can seem to contradict each other, being both happy and sad. How can that be? You may ask: How can I feel both extremes with the same memory? Don't contradictions cancel each other out? If so, would that mean I am left with no feeling?

Not at all. Both feelings are legitimate, real. They both make sense. Yes, we can have positive and negative feelings about the same memory. Just as you can have positive and negative feelings about your partner. You can feel jealous, but still love him or her. You can feel angry, but still want your partner.

You are not confused. No—you are simply aware of how rich and wide-ranging your feelings can be. Because it is never so simple as one feeling, is it? You are filled with all the shapes and colors of the kaleidoscope. Things are one way, and then you spin the wheel. Everything changes in the next moment.

Viewing Your Partner with a Compassion Lens

What are the emotions, other than painful ones, that you and your partner have shared? Is it only jealousy and anger between you? No, it can't be, because if it were you wouldn't care enough to feel jealous. You have shared many other emotions. We were just talking about compassion, loving-kindness, the feeling of being held, caressed, comforted, and totally accepted with all of your human imperfections. Recall that feeling, and try to remember when you experienced it with your partner.

It may feel hard to welcome that feeling, because you are in such pain. But try to bring it back for the moment. Bring it back: to listen, to feel, to remember; to know that this is something that is still up to you; to realize that you can still love each other, even if you are hurting.

In fact, the hurt may be because of your love. Sometimes love hurts; sometimes we are sad because things matter to us. So welcome all those feelings, even when you are hurting. Realize that the pain is there because there are also warm, loving feelings. Even if you want to get rid of your partner to get rid of the hard feelings, you may still love and care for the person who is making you jealous. The pain is only one part of the relationship room. It is surrounded by a whole lot more.

This is the relationship room that you have built together. There is no better time than when you have been hurt to remember the love that you can feel. It's not easy to recall love when you are feeling jealous and angry. So set the jealousy into a chair, over in a corner. Let it rest for a moment so you can now remind yourself of the loving feelings that you have experienced, the love that you have received, the love that you give.

Viewing Your Partner with a Playfulness Lens

As the jealousy sits in the chair, watching, taking it all in, remember once again the playfulness that the two of you have shared: the laughter in times when you were goofy together, just being silly. Yes, you can have these memories by going back in time a little. The jealousy can sit in the chair for now, while you see that those other memories and feelings are also in this relationship room.

Seeing What You Have Solved Together

I want you to remember that something else is in this relationship room: all the problems that you have worked on together. Think back about what you have worked toward, problems that you have solved. Maybe there have been differences, arguments, disappointments lately. But you didn't get here, caring enough to be jealous, if there weren't some problems that you have resolved.

What were they? Maybe you helped each other through difficult times before—through disappointments, problems at work, family struggles, friendship breakdowns. You were there for each other during those times. You were doing it together, not just one person; it was the two of you. Maybe you worked together to raise children, being there at the beginning, at birth, moved so much there were tears in your eyes. Laughing at the kids' antics, watching them grow, waking in the middle of the night, taking turns, together. Maybe you made plans together—activities, vacations, getting things right. Together. Remember all your projects that were about the two of you. Those are still part of this relationship room.

As a Person, You Are More Than Your Jealousy

When you are feeling jealous, you may view the entire relationship as being about jealousy and mistrust. You may even label yourself as "a jealous person." This makes you feel overwhelmed by the jealousy and leads you to be unable to see the richness and diversity of feelings in your relationship—and in yourself.

When you say that you are a jealous person, it's almost as if your entire personality, your entire past history, has disappeared. It's as if you have been replaced with the label. So you begin to cancel yourself out. You are reduced to a diagnosis, a pejorative, a category. You are no longer a distinct person with a unique history and a range of emotions, past relationships, and current relationships. You have placed yourself in a box, closed the lid, and set yourself up on a shelf—perhaps to be discarded.

In fact, at any given moment your relationship and the feelings that you have are far greater than your jealousy. As we have seen, there is a full range of richness to your feelings with each other—joy, happiness, curiosity, closeness—memories of working together on problems, sharing meaningful experiences, planning for the future, and having fun together. Your relationship is larger and richer than your jealous feelings at any given moment. By placing jealousy in the larger context, momentarily letting go of the jealousy, you can learn that there are a variety of possibilities for other feelings and experiences as you focus on the other sources of meaning in your relationship. You are not "a jealous person"—you are a person with a wide range of feelings, experiences, and possibilities.

We can put your jealousy and your relationship in the context of a life larger than the current moment. We can examine how you can build a meaningful life—independent of your current jealousy—that includes friendships, professional relationships, meaningful work, values in life, important goals, and priorities.

Jealous feelings are elements of a larger life, one that is constantly changing, flowing through time, creating new opportunities. You have a life that is larger than your jealousy and it can be filled with a wide range of possibilities—if you unhinge yourself from focusing on jealousy.

Making Space for Everything

Rather than thinking that you need to get rid of your jealous feelings—or the jealous feelings that your partner might have—look at your life as large enough to contain the jealousy...and more. In the relationship room, you can make space for all the feelings. Nothing needs to be banished.

Making room allows us to accept and acknowledge the feelings of jealousy—but it also allows us to make room for the loving, playful, compassionate feelings that are also part of our relationships. When we make room, we no longer struggle against the jealousy, we no longer order it to go away—and we no longer become angry and upset when the jealousy returns. We can accept that "I am feeling a jealous feeling right now" without being upset that it has appeared. We can make room without acting on jealous thoughts and feelings because we can say, "I can accept these feelings for this moment." We say, "I can live with that feeling," knowing that we can add, "and there are a lot of other feelings, memories, and possibilities that I will experience." It's not as if jealousy arrives and empties out the room. It's simply that the jealousy stands up for a moment, cries out in pain, we hear it, and then we continue on. Because making room for how we feel is better than going to war with it.

Chapter 10

Solving It Together

Your experience of jealousy is in the context of the relationship you are in now, in the present moment. Jealousy is seldom a problem for one person. It often involves problematic behavior from both of you. If you are the partner experiencing jealousy, you may have recognized a number of personal problematic patterns of thinking, behaving, communicating, and acting that may have made things even worse at times. This may include mindreading what you think your partner is thinking, withdrawing from her out of spite, interrogating him about his behavior, or labeling her as devious and dishonest. It may or may not be the case that your partner, perhaps unintentionally, has said or done things to trigger those feelings and thoughts, and his or her behavior may be part of the problem. If you are the target of jealousy, you may find yourself labeling your partner as neurotic, defending yourself, and hiding the truth because you don't want to get into more arguments. Both of you take turns trying to be right—trying to win. And you both end up losing.

In this chapter, we will see how the two of you can talk about the jealousy, develop strategies to cope with those feelings, and examine possible ground rules going forward. This may involve some work from both of you to determine what you are agreeing to and what you are signing up for. Sometimes relationships may start with undefined understandings—which are likely to actually be misunderstandings. Sometimes relationships evolve. And sometimes they don't. It will be up to the two of you to decide what will work best for you.

Overall Guidance for Working Together

My experience with couples is that both partners need to contribute to change. It can't simply be one person doing the work and the other person watching it happen. Jealousy is a couple issue, and you can both be part of the solution. It is also an opportunity to dramatically improve mutual understanding and develop guidelines for building greater trust. Rather than fix the blame, you can both focus on finding the solution. Here are some things to keep in mind.

Be Realistic About Expectations

Keep in mind that we need to be realistic about jealousy. As I have said many times in earlier chapters, jealousy is a universal emotion, it is often a statement of commitment, and it is important to accept that it occurs. You are not going to eliminate jealousy—but you can develop an understanding of what drives your jealousy or your responses to your partner's jealousy. In this chapter, we review some powerful tools that you can use to cope with jealousy, as a couple. But understand that having tools to cope with problems doesn't mean you won't have problems. Having them only means that you will know what to do to keep things from escalating. Tools can also offer the opportunity to strengthen your relationship.

The problem is not found in having problems—the problem is found in not having ways to cope. It will be hard at times, you will be discouraged, you might think it's impossible. But your relationship is also worth working on. It may be worth doing some things that feel hard to make it better.

We All Have Baggage

People often say, "I don't want to deal with someone else's baggage." But all of us have some baggage because each of us is imperfect, unfinished. Some of it is light, like carry-on baggage, and some of it is hefty, requiring heavy lifting. Certain things come with the territory: problems with trust, intimacy, misunderstandings, unrealistic expectations, and frustrations. There is no long-term couple with no problems. It takes a lot of work to make relationships work. And working on jealousy together can erupt into accusations and chaos, and it can actually bring you closer— if you do it the right way.

If you expect to have a relationship, you can't escape problems. The key is to be willing to carry each other's baggage. Remember my idea that "I'm not okay, you're not okay—but that's okay" from chapter 6? Well, that may be what we can expect in long-term, meaningful relationships. Whatever baggage you have, or your partner has, depends on the situation. Either of you might have baggage about work, family of origin, money, health, or so many other things. When your partner's jealousy comes, don't think it makes any sense for you to get on a moral high ground, on which you think that your partner's jealousy means you are the better, healthier person. Or, if you are the one experiencing the jealousy, don't assume that you are the only person in the relationship having difficulties. We are all fallen angels. But we can also help each other rise and move along our path together.

Get Beyond Being Right

Don't feel invested in being right all the time. "Being right" is one of the most common problems in relationships. It sets you and your partner up for getting stuck in prosecutor and defendant roles, and one or both play the role of judge. Both of you lose because arguing about being right leads you to attack your partner, defend with self-righteous statements, complain about irrelevant things, and bring up past misunderstandings. Being right is the wrong strategy, even if you are right, because it sabotages the positive goal of building your relationship. Solid relationships are built on mutual reward, understanding, empathy, compassion, and having fun. Being closer, being compassionate, and being vulnerable is how your relationship can flourish. Being right is different from making room for human frailty and failure.

Focus on What's Most Important

Another thing to keep in mind before you and your partner start working on jealousy is that it's important to determine what is worth arguing about and focusing on. Don't approach discussions with the idea that you need to bring up every single disappointment or frustration that you have ever experienced. Psychologists call this kind of thinking "injury collection," and it leads you to go on the offense about the most trivial things. Many of us look for signs that we are being treated unfairly, or focus on slights and insults that may be unintentional or nonexistent. Ask yourself whether you tend to bring up a long laundry list of complaints. Where does doing that get you? Into more arguments. Try to focus only on the most important things. Eliminate the list of injuries. See the larger room of life that you are both living in.

Establish Your Goal for the Discussion

Before you have any discussion, sit down and write out your honest thoughts about what you want to accomplish with it. What is your goal? Consider some examples that have been paired with likely outcomes.

What I Want	What This Might Lead To
"I want to ventilate all my feelings"	Your partner may become defensive, withdraw, or counterattack
"I want to prove that I am right"	Same as above
"I want to make my partner feel as bad as I do"	Same as above
"I want to punish them so they won't do this again"	Same as above
"I want to win the argument"	Same as above
"I want to hold the moral high ground"	Same as above
"I want them to confess and apologize"	Same as above

I think you get the picture. If your goal is simply to ventilate, prove you are right, win the argument, or punish them, then you will get a lot of pushback. When we are in pain, it is natural to try to achieve goals like these—but they only make things worse. When we feel threatened, hurt, and treated unfairly, our first response is to retaliate and express our anger. But it won't accomplish the goal of regaining trust, commitment, and compassion.

Think about it as a *win-win* discussion that also comes with *lose-lose*. No one gets everything that he or she wants, but both of you get something of value. You might get some things that you want, but lose on some other things. It's the same for your partner. Instead of holding out for victory, aim your goal at finding the balance that will move things forward. Think about some of these possible goals.

- I would like to decrease the tension between us

- I would like to build trust

- I would like my partner to respect me

- I would like to feel loved

- I would like to love my partner

- I would like us to understand each other

Before you start difficult discussions, be clear about how you want things to move forward. You may think, "I have to tell her that she is so horrible for making me feel this way" or "I have to get all my feelings out" or "I have a right to my feelings." Ventilating, attacking, or winning may end up escalating into arguments, and turn into defeat for both of you. The questions that will actually help you are "How do I want this to proceed?" and "What outcome am I looking for?" So let's think about a better strategy. Let's begin with *listening*.

Approaching the Discussion

Try to step away from your desire to win the argument and instead think about what is more important in your relationship: being right or being happier together? Your discussion about jealousy obviously will involve facts, logic, and fairness, but it will also involve both of you feeling heard, respected, and valued. Each person comes to the relationship with a past history: for example, one of you may have a history of betrayal, or one of you might have a history of not committing fully. You both have your own assumptions, and may feel entitled to certain behavior or feel you should be treated a certain way. But your discussion is not a trial; it's not a debate. Remember that there are no winners and losers here. It's not "I'm right, you're wrong" because making the discussion into a contest will guarantee that both of you will be unhappy. The discussion needs to focus on mutual understanding, mutual respect, mutual collaboration. It's about listening and sharing, not about dominating and controlling. It's an attempt to get closer by opening up some vulnerabilities that both of you may have. It's not "I win, he loses"; rather, it's "I listened, she listened." So start with trying to understand your partner's point of view by considering his or her thoughts, feelings, and vulnerabilities.

Consider Your Partner's Point of View

Here is a simple exercise for both of you to do. Write down how you think your partner sees the issues in the relationship. What do you think he or she would say about them? I have found that taking this first step, before you start unloading your anger and anxiety, can open your eyes to two possibilities. First, you have no idea how your partner sees things. Second, when you start thinking about it, you realize that he or she is seeing things a lot differently than you are.

Show Your Partner You Are Listening

Next, step away from winning the argument to temporarily join your partner on his or her side. This can involve rephrasing what you hear him saying, so he can realize that you at least hear him.

Let Your Partner Know You Understand

Then try to find some truth in what she is saying, like "I can understand that you might feel jealous when I am around women who flirt with me" or "I can understand that my jealousy makes you feel that you are being unfairly attacked."

Why is it important to understand and show respect for the other person's point of view? Why is it important to step away from *trying to win* and step into *trying to understand*? In some ways, it is quite simple. Jealousy is about threats to attachment—threats to your bond—so when you discuss it, keep in mind that you can strengthen the bond by helping each other feel heard. Jealousy is like crying out and not being heard. So when you strengthen the attachment by improving mutual understanding, and build compassion by validating and respecting, then you will feel more secure and less prone to jealousy. If you want to be heard, you need to listen to the other person. In order to be heard, we first must listen.

The key point is to create a *safe space for sharing feelings*. Jealousy reflects the fear that you are not safe. Imagine that you and your partner are in a dark cave where there are different passages, but neither of you knows the way out. It is dark and the two of you are alone. You are holding a candle that flickers in the darkness, and it is important to keep this candle lit because without it there is no way out. You hold this candle together to help you find your way. Imagine that this candle is your jealousy and that you can walk together, holding it, looking for more light through one of those passages. It is your candle, it is what you are sharing together, and you must rely on each other to find the way. Think of your discussions as the candle's light.

Consider Your Own Beliefs About Jealousy

Examine your beliefs and assumptions that inadvertently result in problematic or provocative behavior. These assumptions and rule-books, which I covered in chapter 4, can get in the way of a productive discussion in which you can work on the relationship and simultaneously find room for the jealousy. These include the following: "Men are different from women," "No one can tell me what to do," "I shouldn't have to deal with this," or "This will never change."

You can also examine any anti-jealousy beliefs that serve as judgments of your partner. These include beliefs like "My partner shouldn't be jealous," "Only people who are insecure feel jealous," and "She should just trust me." Ask yourself whether these beliefs are helping in the relationship. Probably not.

We are often motivated to view ourselves as well-meaning, good people whose behavior should never be questioned. And you may be well-meaning. But the idea that your partner should "just trust me" sounds like you are entitled to those feelings, no matter what. Many of us believe we have an *entitlement* to getting things our way, while denying problems that both partners contribute to. Consider more balanced and realistic beliefs that can allow you to accept your partner's jealous feelings while helping your partner cope more effectively with the struggle that he or she is facing. It takes two to deal with jealousy. These helpful beliefs include:

- Jealousy is a problem in a lot of relationships

- We can both accept that jealousy is a normal emotion for people and that we can both have compassion for each other, even where there is jealousy

- Relationships require compromise and balance—no one gets everything exactly the way he or she wants it

- How the two of us communicate about the jealousy will help us cope better with it

Ground Rules for the Discussion

Think about the discussion as a *conference time* and limit its length. When talking about jealousy, it is important to find a neutral time when neither of you is particularly upset. For example, you might begin by saying, "Let's sit down for no more than twenty minutes to begin our discussion about how we can both cope with jealousy in our relationship. Let's try to focus on understanding how each of us feels."

Own Up to Your Role in the Problem

Don't think of the discussion as an opportunity to prosecute your partner and judge him or her. By sharing some role in the problem, it becomes "This is our problem, not your problem." It allows the two of you to work together. You can say, "I know that I contribute to the problem, so I want to be a part of helping us find some solutions." Think about it as mutual problem-solving to talk about how you can build more trust and what you can do to help.

Present the jealousy as a problem to *solve* and a problem to *share*. For example, if you are the one experiencing jealousy, you can start by saying, "I know that my jealousy must upset you almost as much as it upsets me. I know that this is part of our problem together. So I would like to understand more about how you experience it, and I would like to tell you more about how I experience it." If you are the target of the jealousy, you can say, "I know that there may be some things that I say or do that may not be intentional on my part, but that may upset you. So I would like to hear about how it feels to you, and I would like you to know more about how I feel. But I can see that it is hard for both of us."

My observation is that often it takes two to have a jealousy problem. Sometimes we may do things that we think are innocent, even well-intentioned, but that elicit jealousy in our partner. For example, you may have coffee with an ex-partner, or send greetings on social media to someone you were once involved with. Your intention was to be friendly, but you weren't thinking of how your partner would experience it. So you respond with self-righteous disbelief, with "What is wrong with you? I wasn't doing anything!" Or sometimes your partner can respond to your jealousy with anger and ridicule, which only makes the problem worse. By accepting that *this is our problem because this is our relationship*, you can work to respect each other more while listening. It takes two to solve *our* problem.

Avoid Labeling Each Other

Any discussion that involves labeling the other person as neurotic, insecure, selfish, or narcissistic is not likely to end well. Avoid these pejoratives and generalizations. Instead, you can say, "Let's first try to understand how we each are experiencing this." When we label people, they feel humiliated and marginalized—which makes them unlikely to consider any change. And, once labeled, they will want to counterattack or withdraw. Solving the jealousy problem should be about bringing you closer, not blaming one person. No one gets closer by being labeled "insecure" or "neurotic."

Give Each Other Time to Talk—Uninterrupted

You don't want to have either one of you taking the floor and lecturing because the other person will tune out. So agree to give each other five minutes to express thoughts and feelings. While your partner has his five minutes of talking, your job is to write down the major points—whether you agree with him or not. For example, let's say that your female partner says, "I feel really anxious when you are around other women whom I think you find attractive. I think you enjoy their company and I think you enjoy flirting with them." Whether you agree or not, write down what you hear. At the end of the five minutes, you can say (among other things), "Let me see if I got your point of view. It sounds like you feel uncomfortable when I am around other women and you think that I enjoy flirting with them. Am I understanding your point of view so far?" This allows each of you to express your views without being criticized and without arguing. It allows both of you to be heard. Hearing what your partner says does not mean that you agree with what he or she is saying. It only means that you got the information, which strengthens the bond. The candle gets brighter.

Direct Some Compassion Toward Your Partner

You are both taking some time to share painful and difficult feelings, so it would be a good idea to step back, direct some compassion and kindness toward your partner, and appreciate him or her for speaking and listening. Even though you may be anxious or angry, allowing compassion to enter the room can help calm both of you down.[47] After all, you are having this discussion because you want things to be better. You can direct compassion by saying, "I appreciate your efforts to talk with me about this, because I know it causes both of us some difficulty. I can see that this is hard for you at times, and I truly want you to feel better because I care about you. I know this whole issue is a hard one, so I want to bring some peace and trust to our relationship." When you express and experience compassion, there is warmth in the room. It is feeling safer.

Identify What You Want Your Partner to Do

After you have given each other sufficient time to be heard, think through what you want your partner to do differently. For example, are you going to ask your partner never to talk to other women or men? Would this be realistic? Is there some change in behavior that you are looking for? You may have some difficulty specifying a change that you want to see. But it's important because while you may be angry with your partner, even agreeing to small changes moves things forward and builds more trust.

Identify What You Agree On

Many discussions seem to focus on the points of disagreement. But as you discuss jealousy, you can widen the discussion to some of the good things in your relationship. Think about the relationship room that we discussed in the previous chapter. Think about all the good things that you have shared. Talking about what you agree on can begin with discussing some of the good things in the relationship. For example, Dave had a lot of jealous feelings about Laura and her male colleagues. So he followed my suggestion and talked about the things that he valued in Laura:

> "I know that you are a terrific mother to our children. You really take an interest in their schoolwork, you put a lot of effort into listening to them, and you talk with them when they have problems. I can see that you really love them and that they love you. And I can also see how hard you work at the office. You are juggling a lot of things as you work at the office and try to be a good mom."

Then Dave continued to talk about what they agreed on.

> "I agree with you that I have a lot of jealous feelings at times, and I can make it difficult for you with my questions and my anxiety. I think we agree that this has become a problem for the two of us and that we both would like to have fewer arguments. I also know that there are times when I have been unfair with you."

Laura was able to talk about what she valued in Dave.

> "I know that you are also doing a lot to help with the kids and that you work hard too. I know that you love them and I know you love me. And I appreciate that there are times when you take on some more responsibilities when I have business trips, which can be a burden for you."

Then Laura identified what they did agree on.

> "I agree with you that the jealousy has become a problem for both of us and I can see that it eats you alive. You seem so anxious, angry, and a little lost with your jealousy. I know that it gets between us. I agree that this is

something we need to work on. And to be honest, I know that there are times that I might do things that make you uncomfortable. Like at the office party, when Ted put his arm around me and I didn't move away from it even though I knew that it was going to piss you off. So I can see that there may be things that I do to contribute to this. I agree that I am not entirely blameless here."

How to Communicate Your Jealousy to Your Partner

If you are the one feeling jealous, you can do six things to help your discussion along. Use this list as a quick guide for conveying your feelings.

1. Acknowledge that you have a jealousy problem

2. Validate that this has a negative effect on your partner

3. Direct compassion toward the accused partner

4. Ask for direction: "When I am feeling jealous, how should I communicate that to you so that you don't feel accused?"

5. See whether your partner can validate and comfort you

6. Agree that you can feel jealous without taking action

Be Honest with Yourself About Your Behavior

There are times when people intentionally try to make their partners feel jealous. It can serve many purposes. Here are a few. Instigating jealousy can be:

- A way of testing a partner

- A method of punishing him or her for something

- A competition if he or she is flirting with someone

- A way to hedge bets, flirting with others to ensure an alternative should the current relationship end

- A boost to self-esteem, to prove they are still attractive

- A way to prove that no one can tell them what to do

You can ask yourself, "What kinds of things could I do that provoke jealousy in my partner?" Then, ask yourself whether this conflict is worth it to support your behavior. I said it before, and I'll say it again: it often takes two to have a jealousy problem.

Think About What You Would Be Willing to Change

We almost always want our partner to be the one to change, but things are likely to work a lot better if we also become agents of change. You might think about this before you sit down to have your discussion. You can list a few things that you anticipate your partner would like you to change, and think about which of these might be worth some effort on your part. Then when you have your discussions, you can find out whether you guessed correctly. Did you actually know what your partner wanted you to do?

Listen to what your partner has been complaining about and think of it as a menu of change. For example, if your partner complains that you are constantly interrogating her, consider giving that up. If your partner complains that you accuse him of things that he hasn't done, then consider giving up the role of being a prosecutor. And, if you are the target of jealousy, consider what you would be willing to change. One difficulty may be that you are reluctant to be honest with your jealous partner because you fear that you will be criticized. So you may hide interactions with others, mostly to avoid that criticism. Of course, when such secret meetings are discovered, it only inflames the situation. If you want to build trust, you need to work at transparency and honesty, even if it is unpleasant for you.

> Nick secretly had drinks a number of times with other women, and his wife, Carol, found out when she saw a text message on his phone. So Carol grew distrustful and wondered what else she didn't know. At first, Nick tried to explain that these meetings were innocent, that they were related to business (which they really weren't in some cases), and that he had a right to some relaxation time because his wife is so work-absorbed that she seldom has time for him.

None of these responses worked because all they did was dig a deeper hole for distrust to grow. Nick and I talked about the pros and cons of these "flirtations," and he realized that the few minutes of ego boosting that he got from the company of these women did not compare to how much he valued his relationship with Carol. Yes, he might have some reasons to complain about Carol being work-absorbed. We could work on that as a separate issue, but first he needed to consider working on rebuilding trust. When he finally realized that regaining trust was going to take some effort, he decided to agree with Carol about some guidelines. He said to her:

> "Okay, I can understand why it would upset you that I met her for drinks, so here is what I would like to propose. If I do have plans to get together with a business associate for drinks or dinner, I will let you know in advance so you won't feel I am hiding anything."

Because Nick did have legitimate reasons for meeting men and women in his business, he needed to consider how honest he was going to be with Carol. He also realized that telling Carol the truth might lead to some arguments, and part of him wanted to avoid any conflict. He was tempted to continue finding ways to get away with these secret meetings. But then he realized that trying to compartmentalize his life with secret meetings, while simultaneously trying to build trust with Carol, was not going to work. I said, "I know a lot of people think that they can juggle a lot of relationships and keep them separate. I can also see that flirtation with some of these women might be exciting for you. But I have also seen in my work that keeping life simple is the less stressful way to go. Ask yourself, 'How would Carol feel if she knew that this was happening?' If the answer is that she would be upset, then you need to question whether it is worth it to you or not."

Navigating What Freedom Is to You

Most of us don't like being told what to do. We think that we should be trusted and respected just the way we are. If we want to see other people on our terms, then we should be able to do that. This idea of total freedom might work if you are not in a relationship, if you are simply dating around, having casual hookups and no commitments. You need to decide what the nature of your relationship is going to be. Are you going to develop commitment or are you simply going to do whatever you want to do? You need to be aware of this choice. If you are in a relationship where both of you have made a commitment, then you need to ask yourself what you are willing to give up in order to keep that commitment.

Couples differ in what freedoms they are willing to accept. There are no hard and set rules. Agreeing on the level of freedom involves an open discussion of what you are willing to change and willing to accept. It doesn't mean that a partner has to comply with every request you have. But there may be reasonable compromises that you can reach. I know a couple who have been married for many years. The wife likes to go out dancing and the husband has no interest. He trusts her and isn't worried that she dances with other men. They have been doing this for many years without any affairs or major conflicts. Most other couples would have a great deal of difficulty with this. There is no hard and fast rule.

Think of freedom this way: if you are free to have shallow, superficial relationships, then what you will experience is a shallow, superficial life. If you are able to make a lasting commitment and build trust, you are free to experience depth, commitment, shared history, and a future that you both rely on. What freedom is for you is related to the goals that you value. If you value the freedom to have casual relationships, then you will achieve the goal of superficial, temporary relationships. If your goal is deep and lasting commitment, then freedom carries responsibilities in your relationship. The freedom to achieve trust and commitment involves the responsibility to build them. Neither just happens.

One day Nick came into my office, sat down on the couch, and began to cry intensely. "I don't want to lose my wife and my child. I can't believe I was so stupid." He was feeling devastated because his wife found out about his flirtatious text messages with a woman. He realized his marriage was at stake, and that in order to have the freedom to have a trusting relationship with Carol, to live with his wife and child in peace, he would have to reexamine other freedoms. This included the freedom to see other women for drinks and secret flirtations. It turns out that *freedom isn't free.*

Some people think that they should be able to do whatever they want, and that their partner should accept it. The consequence is a series of broken relationships in which trust has eroded. This leads to the next relationship where trust will erode again. Ron White is a rather raunchy comedian who recalls an experience in his life: "The great thing about not cheating is that you never get caught."[48] Simplicity is often the key to a meaningful life.

Relationships require decisions. You both need to think about the trade-offs you are willing to accept. Like a lot of things in life, *there is no free lunch*. If you are the one feeling jealous, then you might make a list of the behaviors that trigger your jealousy and order them: what you absolutely cannot accept, what you could accept with some discomfort, and what you could accept more easily.

As a target of jealousy, you may need to examine your beliefs about what commitment means. For each behavior that you are having difficulty accepting or changing, write out the reasons for your belief. Think of your relationship as something you value, something that requires flexibility, and something that you are willing to work on.

Ways to Respond to Your Jealous Partner

It's not just the jealousy that is the problem; it's also how the two of you talk about it. When you feel accused, it's natural to defend, counterattack, proclaim your innocence, or withdraw further. No one likes to be accused, interrogated, or distrusted. After all, you are only human and you believe that your partner is being unfair with you—even hostile. But his or her feelings are genuine, painful, and lonely. This person is someone you love, who loves you and fears losing you.

Your innocence is not really the issue. It's the difficulty that your partner has coping with these intense feelings about someone they love and fear losing. If your partner is jealous, you can decide to approach this with understanding, compassion, and respect. How you respond to the jealousy—how both of you respond—will determine whether you are driven further away from each other or, with a lot of work and compassion, you two grow closer, more trusting, and more trustworthy.

Before you throw your arms in the air and give up, consider joining with your partner to see whether this can become a turning point to improve listening and being heard, solving problems together, and sharing compassionate feelings. What do you have to lose by trying?

Think of it this way: Your partner is feeling overwhelmed with anxiety, anger, and fears that you are losing interest. He or she may lash out at you because this may be the only way your partner knows how to act at present. Stand back to observe and accept. Your partner is struggling. Here are some suggestions for how to be with him or her.

- Recognize that he will feel jealous for the time being, and accept that for the moment

- Show an interest in her feelings

- Express compassion in a way that assures him you care about how difficult this is

- Rephrase what you hear—you don't need to agree with her to hear things accurately

- Find some points of validity, like you can understand why he might be distrustful

- Own up to some role in the problem

- Normalize that other people have the same feelings

- Recognize that these emotions your partner has at the moment will pass

- Think about all the other positive emotions and experiences that you two share

- Don't try to convince your partner to change the way he feels—accept it as an expression of where he is at the moment

- Assure her that you are here for her, even if you acknowledge that she is angry with you

Some partners are reluctant to modify their behavior because they may honestly not be doing anything that involves betrayal. That is understandable. But relationships often require us to think about what we might be willing to do to honor the feelings and needs of our partners. This discussion can be an ongoing one.

Keep Working with It

Don't assume that jealousy will go away. It doesn't have to. Keep the relationship room in mind, where there are many memories, thoughts, feelings, and experiences in the past, present, and future. It is constantly growing and changing. Make room for the jealousy so that you can accept that these feelings may come and go. Also keep in mind all the other parts of the relationship room.

As you work together, for a while set aside the jealousy and work at planning things together. Sometimes we get stuck on a painful feeling like jealousy and we keep ruminating about it. But you can accept that the feeling may be there, even every day at times, but you can still plan things together.

Dave and Laura had been so focused on Dave's jealousy that they weren't doing many positive things together. I suggested that, to build the bond in the marriage, it made sense to have fun doing things together. Dave realized that he wanted to build the relationship, even though he felt jealous, but he thought, "How could I do things with her when she has hurt me like this?" I suggested that he accept he had good reasons to feel jealous, but there were lots of other feelings he had toward his wife, like love, sexual desire, and enjoying her companionship. Just because she gave him good reasons for jealousy didn't mean that he needed to give up relating to her. I suggested we try *opposite action*—that is, rather than expressing his hostility and distrust, he could try expressing his love and affection. This was hard for Dave because he thought that he had a right to his feelings—which he did. But he also had a right to change his feelings and make the relationship better. So he and his wife planned dinners together, shopping, sensual pleasure, sharing meals at home, and watching videos of TV shows that they liked. As the positive bond strengthened for the two of them, the intensity of his jealousy diminished.

Even when you have been hurt, even when you have good reasons for your jealousy, it doesn't mean that you need to give up. You can keep making things better even after they have gotten worse. You might call that progress.

Jealousy doesn't have to be the end of your relationship. If the two of you use it as an opportunity to listen, communicate, support, accept, and show compassion for one another, your relationship can turn in a new direction. It can build greater trust, understanding, and commitment. Rather than drive the two of you apart, understanding your jealousy can help you heal the agony and fear that has led the two of you in the wrong direction. Jealousy is part of being a human being, it's part of intimacy, and it's a statement that you value commitment and honesty. If you can carry the candle together, turning fear into compassion, then your bond can become stronger. It will take a lot of work. It won't be easy. But if the two of you work together, the baggage is not as heavy and the candle's flame burns, warm and bright.

Getting Past the Past to Overcome Retrospective Jealousy

Josh is anxious about going to a party where he knows Molly's former boyfriend, Emmon, will be. It makes him both worried and angry, and he doesn't know how he will handle it. All he can think of is that Molly had sex with Emmon, which makes him furious with jealousy. He knows that Molly broke it off with Emmon because she thought Emmon was too controlling and critical. She tells Josh that she has no desire to get back together with Emmon. But this isn't enough for Josh. "If I see him, I know that I will want to punch him in the face." He knows that this isn't the right thing to do, and that it has been over between Molly and Emmon for six months, but the feelings are too intense for him right now.

It's hard to imagine any of us without a past filled with romance, sensuality, and attachment to someone else. We are not living in a world of vestal virgins and universal chastity. But many people are plagued by thoughts and images of the former lovers of their current partners. Many people think about this former partner and are upset about the idea that they were sexually intimate, or in love, with that person.

If you have this experience, you may compare yourself with that other person, whom you have never met. You think things like "I wonder how much he enjoyed sex with her," "He probably loved her more than he loves me," "He must be thinking about her and comparing me with her." In this comparison, you may think your partner may still love that person, want to be with that person, or fantasize about that person.

In this chapter, we will examine how getting stuck on jealousy about past relationships can hijack you and keep you from enjoying the present moment. We will look at examples of this retrospective jealousy, how it is tied in with perfectionism and illusions about purity, and how you can use a number of powerful techniques right now to live in the present while accepting that the past is background. You don't have to be *the only one* who ever existed for your partner to be the true one at the present moment. Look at the following statements and see whether any of these fit you.

- I often think about the fact that my current partner had a lover in the past

- When I think about this, I feel uneasy—anxious and worried

- I wonder whether my current partner had a better relationship with his or her former lover

- I want to be the only person that my partner ever enjoyed and had passion with

If any of these statements rings true, then you might find yourself caught up in *retrospective jealousy*. Even if your current relationship is going well, you might dwell on your partner's past relationships, comparing yourself with them, and feeling anxious and angry about it. In this chapter, we will look at how this rumination, anxiety, and anger might make sense to your jealous mind.

And we will look at a number of techniques you can use now to reverse getting stuck on the past. After all, in order to enjoy the present moment, you will need to leave the past behind you.

"I Want to Be the Only One"

It may seem natural to believe that your partner could only desire you, or to think your partner could only have good sex with you. Part of the romantic ideal is that we are special and *exclusively* special to our partners. We believe at times that our partners should not find anyone else attractive while we are with them and, in the case of retrospective jealousy, we may harbor the belief that no one has been attractive to them in the past. This is *romantic perfectionism*, in which there is something unique about our current relationship that requires, in our minds, that all past relationships should never have existed. We become obsessed with purity, as if our current partners have been spoiled by their past behavior. But holding this assumption will only make us miserable. Let's look at its logic by asking a series of questions.

- Why should your partner not have had enjoyable sex with someone else in the past?

- Is it because you expect that he could only be attracted to you?

- Do you think that you are the only person who could arouse her? Why would that be?

- Why should you be the only sexy person in the world?

- Is your partner the only person that you have ever found attractive or enjoyed sex with?

- Does that mean that you can't be trusted? Does this seem realistic?

- Doesn't it make sense that people who have been sexually active would have enjoyed sex with other people?

- After all, you probably enjoyed sex with other people. Does that mean that your partner should feel threatened too?

It's almost as if you think you should be the only person in the entire world that your partner could desire. Imagine if that were true. Of the six billion people in the world, your partner would only be able to have satisfaction with you. It's almost as if your current partner was going along in life for twenty or thirty years, and no one was attractive to them—until you came along and everything changed.

This is what I call *desire perfectionism*, which is the idea that your partner should only have ever had desire for you and no one else. We often use desire perfectionism when we think about a partner's past experiences, and also about potential fantasies or desires that our partners may have today. This is based on the *purity illusion*, the idea that true love requires purity and celibacy. It's an illusion because adults in today's world are freed from the strictures of religious and cultural taboos that have often been used to punish, even kill, women. We are living in the twenty-first century, after all.

New Ways to View Your Jealousy

Let's look further at the logic of this. Say you and your future partner are both thirty years old. You are just meeting. Your new acquaintance tells you, "I am thirty years old and I have never been sexually attracted to anyone in the world. I have dated various men (women) and no one appealed to me. But I just noticed that I am feeling turned on to you!"

What would you think? First, you might think that this person is lying about the past. Or you might think there is something dreadfully wrong with him or her if they had never been attracted or aroused by anyone. You might wonder: Are they severely depressed? Are they unsure about sexual orientation? Does he or she have some medical condition? And, if any of those conditions accounted for a lack of previous sexual desire, what would you predict about the future? Will this desire for you be reliable? This may start to seem unrealistic. But it may be exactly how you think, with your purity illusions and desire perfectionism.

Put the Shoe on Your Own Foot

Let's look at your own experience. Were there people you desired, and found sexual satisfaction with, before you met your current partner? Should you feel guilty about that? Maybe it simply means that you have had healthy, normal past experiences with other people. So should your current partner distrust you?

After all, think about your past and the experiences that you enjoyed. Wasn't it fun? Ask yourself whether this means that you can't love, and commit to, your current partner. Maybe pleasure with past partners means that you cannot control yourself now. Are you constantly going back to past partners and having sex with them? Why not? Perhaps because the past *is the past* for you.

> Josh had many former lovers, but he is worried about Molly's former lover appearing at the party. When I ask him if she should be concerned about his past relationships, he gets defensive: "Why should she be concerned? I love her! Those relationships are over." I ask him if that might also be true for Molly. Her past relationships are just that—in the past, over. Josh pauses for a moment and says reluctantly, "I guess you have a point. She has as much to worry about as I do."

After all, most relationships end, often because one person, or both partners, think it's no longer worth it. When your past relationships ended, they opened the possibility for your current relationship.

The Hidden Rules for Retrospective Jealousy

Although it's not unusual for us to have some jealousy about our partner's past relationships, some people are very perplexed and hijacked by the past. When we explore the thinking behind this retrospective jealousy, we find a number of relationship rule-books that magnify it. Consider the possibility that it's not the past that is upsetting—it's your rules that are upsetting. Here are some examples of these rule-books.

- I should be the only person my partner ever desired

- If my partner enjoyed sex with someone else, then he might go back to that person

- If she enjoyed sex with someone else, then she will leave me for another person

- It's dangerous to my current relationship if my partner has fond memories about a past partner

Imagine that you believe one or more of these retrospective jealousy rules. What will happen? You will feel frustrated, even defeated, by an impossible scenario. You will continually worry about your partner leaving you for a past lover or for someone else in the future. Because you feel threatened by the past, you will find yourself testing your partner, interrogating him, trying to limit her behavior. Because the past will never disappear, you will be stuck in something you can never change.

An Evolutionary Lens

A different way to look at past desires and relationships is to view them from an evolutionary perspective. Desire has evolved because it has been adaptive to the species. Having desire for many other people is adaptive because it allowed our ancestors to procreate. If a target of desire were limited to one person, per person, and a desirable other never came along, then there would be no procreation. In the context of evolution, it's somewhat absurd to think that you would be the only person your partner could desire or feel satisfaction with.

You may believe that your partner's past—or current–desire will inevitably lead to action. Josh asked me, "If Molly desired Emmon, then what's to keep her from going back to him or getting involved with someone else?" I observed that Josh thought Molly's desire, memory, and even fantasy life were dangerous to him. He believed she would be overpowered with desire, and would not be able to control herself. This is like the *thought-action fusion* we described earlier: "If Molly has a desire, then she will act on it." I suggested we test this out with himself.

Bob: How often do you see women you feel attracted to?

Josh: (*Smiling*) Every day.

Bob: Since you have been involved with Molly, how many times have you chosen to be unfaithful?

Josh: Never.

Bob: Doesn't this suggest that there is often a disconnect between having a desire or a fantasy and acting on it?

Josh: Yes.

Bob: So why haven't you acted on your fantasies and desires?

Josh: I can see another woman is attractive, and even fanta-size about her, but I really love Molly. Acting on those thoughts would just screw things up. I don't want to make my life more complicated. It's just not worth it.

Bob: Is it possible that the same process of reflection and choice might also be true for Molly? While she might recall sex with Emmon, even having some fond sensual feelings, she might decide that it simply is not worth it. Is it possible that there is a big difference between having a thought or feeling, and making a choice to engage in a behavior? Isn't this what you do every day?

Nathan is a happily married man. He was worried about his marriage—and about himself—because he noticed that he was attracted to young women in Starbucks. It was the late spring, so a lot of women were wearing revealing clothing. He found this sexy, but then worried, "There must be something wrong with my marriage if I find these women sexy." I asked him what he was worried would happen.

Nathan: I am worried that I might lose control and start having an affair with one of them.

Bob: Why haven't you? Let's walk through the steps: You see an attractive woman, you start talking with her, you find that you hit it off, you start seeing her secretly, you hide this from your wife, you get two phones—one for your business and the other for your new lover—you see your new lover in a hotel room, this goes on for months...

Nathan: I would never do that!

Bob: Why not? Didn't you tell me that you desire some of these women?

Nathan: (*With even more intensity*) I would never want to make my life complicated like that. I would never hurt my wife and children.

I suggested that this illustrates clearly how we can have fantasies and desires, and then make choices that go against them because something else is more important—in this case, a marriage.

Establishing Realistic Guidelines

Now that we have looked at these relationship rules, let's rewrite some more realistic and livable guidelines that won't destroy your current relationship. Here are some suggestions.

- I should not be the only person my partner ever desired

- If my partner enjoyed sex with someone else, then it means nothing about the possibility that he might go back to that person

- If my partner enjoyed sex with someone else, then she can also enjoy sex with me

- It's not dangerous to my current relationship if my partner has fond memories about a past partner. It's natural for all of us to reflect on positive experiences in the past. That's what memories are for.

"If My Partner Wanted Him, How Can She Want Me?"

Let's look at your either-or, black-and-white, dichotomous thinking. It goes something like this: "If my partner has a desire for someone else, in the past or present, then it means that he doesn't have any desire for me." This is a form of desire perfectionism, in which you can only have one desire, and this desire cancels out all other desires.

We'll think this through by talking about food. Let's say you really love a particular pasta dish with lobster and red sauce. You just love it. But the restaurant sold the last lobster. So the waiter tells you that they have a delicious eggplant parmesan on the menu, along with thirty other great options. Do you say, "How can you talk about anything else besides the lobster with red sauce?" and walk out of the restaurant?

Similarly, your partner might have had desires for someone else in the past, but that relationship ended. Maybe they both decided that they couldn't stand each other. But it may also be true that your partner occasionally has a fond memory of the past with this person—perhaps selectively remembering a good time. Does this mean that her desire and fantasy prevents her from having desire for you in the present moment? Desires and fantasies are not either-or. They don't cancel each other out. You might find yourself having a fantasy about another person but also enjoying intimacy with your partner. Both can exist, side by side.

"Maybe the Other Person Was a Better Lover Than Me"

Let's look at your fear that your partner might think that a former lover was more satisfying. What if that were true? This was one of Josh's fears.

Josh: I don't know exactly what it was like for Molly and Emmon, but I worry sometimes that she might have thought he was a better lover than I am.

Bob: What would that mean if it were true? Does it necessarily mean your partner cannot be satisfied with you?

Does every experience have to be the very best in order to be satisfying?

Josh: *(Thinking for a moment)* The sensual relationship with Molly is generally pretty good, but there are times when she is too tired or not interested. When this happens, I wonder whether she is losing interest and will start comparing our relationship with what she had with Emmon.

Josh was suffering from *sensual perfectionism*, a belief that the only kind of sensual experience that could be satisfying is the perfect experience. Based on that, he was assuming Molly had that with someone else in the past, and that she could only be happy with sensual perfection.

Let's look at this with a trivial example. Imagine that five years ago you went to the best restaurant in the world and ate the best meal of your entire life. Does that mean you never ate another meal you enjoyed after that? Perhaps it would be more accurate to say that you've had many meals since then, and you will have many more in the future, that are very enjoyable and satisfying. The "best" does not have to be the enemy of *all the rest*.

Say the only experience you can find satisfying is the very best you can have in your entire life. Imagine that your best sexual experience happened five years ago. Given the logic of this perfectionism, you would never be satisfied or happy with any experience thereafter. The rest of your experiences are unsatisfactory and make you miserable. Does this really make sense? Can there be a wide range of satisfying and rewarding experiences that are not the absolute best experiences ever? Let's imagine a conversation between two people who love each other and just had sex.

Man: That was really terrific. How about for you?

Woman: Really nice. I enjoyed myself too.

Man:	Was it the best sex you ever had in your entire life?
Woman:	I can't really say, but it was really good.
Man:	What? You mean that you had better sex with someone else?
Woman:	I don't recall, but I guess that's possible.
Man:	Well, that's something I can't live with. Your sex with me must be the best you have ever had, each and every time. It has to be better than before.
Woman:	Isn't that unrealistic?
Man:	What, don't you love me?
Woman:	Of course I do, but this sounds crazy to me.

Maybe the woman in this dialogue has a point. Demanding perfection, and the very best, is an absurd standard to use. Experiences can range in terms of pleasure and, in fact, if you have pleasurable experiences frequently it makes no difference what happened five years ago. Sex is about pleasure in the current moment, not setting world records that hold up for years.

"I Can't Get This Out of My Mind"

Many people who suffer from retrospective jealousy seem to dwell on the imagined, past experiences of their current partner. They ruminate about how exciting and meaningful a partner's past experiences were and conclude that this must interfere with the current relationship. Take a look at the following statements and ask yourself whether any ring true.

- I often think about the fact that my partner enjoyed sex with other people before he met me

- I can't get these thoughts out of my mind

- When I think about the past that she enjoyed, it upsets me

- I keep dwelling on the possibility that he is thinking about those past experiences

- If my partner does think about those past experiences, then it means that our relationship is flawed—even doomed

Perhaps some, or all, of these thoughts ring true for you. You find yourself stuck on these thoughts and you may form images in your mind about your partner's past. You may think that because you are having these thoughts, something very meaningful—and bad—has happened. Your current relationship is, in some sense, stained by the past. You may even think that, because your partner had these experiences, you are second best, a consolation prize, and you can't accept this. You cannot tolerate these intrusive thoughts. You have to get rid of them in order to enjoy your current relationship. You try to push these thoughts out of your mind—but they keep plaguing you, nagging you, and they hijack you. Wherever you go, the thoughts follow you.

What if you were to accept that you have these thoughts and images? They could be perfectly natural curiosities. You could try seeing them as simply part of the *collective memory* of your relationship: just as you think these things, your partner may also have thoughts and images about your past experiences. Consider whether this might simply be a natural part of relationships, as the past is often part of our curiosity about the person we are currently with. As you accept these thoughts, you can use mindful detachment. Simply point to them and say the following:

"Ah, so there is another thought about my partner's past. I just noticed that my mind sent that thought out and I can see it right here. It's interesting how my mind works, sending out thoughts and images. I can accept those thoughts, they are natural, everyone has them, and I can observe them and realize that they are *just thoughts*. I can bring my attention back to the present moment. I can notice my breath going in and out. I can breathe in the thought, 'He had a past partner,' and breathe out, 'I let that go.' These are moment-to-moment thoughts, mental events, things in my brain. I don't have to get rid of them; I can just live along with them."

Begin practicing mindful detachment: standing back, observing, accepting, not trying to control these thoughts, not judging them. As you do, you may notice that these thoughts become more fluid, flowing back and forth, without hijacking you. You may begin to notice that you can live in a world where these thoughts occur, you don't need to get rid of them, and you don't have to spend a lot of time thinking about them. They are just thoughts.

Remind yourself that your current relationship is in the *present moment*. You can turn to your partner with warmth, love, and compassion—even when you have thoughts and images about the past.

Arriving at the Present Moment

What if you were to radically accept the past? Could it be a *given fact* that your partner was attracted to other people and enjoyed sex with them? When we radically accept something, we neither judge it nor control it, and we simply try to live with it as a fact about *what is*. What is—*is*. What was—*was*. *Here is now.*

The past is what you accept with this question: "Given the past, what can I still do in the present moment with my partner?" Well, you can have a rewarding, intimate, meaningful relationship. You can make moments together special. This is your moment with him. This is her moment with you. It's not the only moment in your life, but it is the current moment—and that is where the rewards are. So here are some ways to arrive at the present.

Shifting Your Focus to Now

Look around you right now. At the present moment, what do you see right around you? Focus on one thing, one object, and describe it to yourself. I am looking at an abstract painting. I see gray shapes and some beige color and a dark area at the bottom. It is a painting of reflections of windows. It is my present moment, at this moment. Shifting your focus to the present moment can be this simple as you leave the past where it is.

Letting Go of the Past

You have struggled against the past for a while, and imagine that you now think, "I will try to give up on my partner's past. I will try to live in the present." But you also notice that thoughts about his or her past keep plaguing you, keep nagging you, and you find yourself hijacked by them.

What I want you to imagine, at the present moment, is that these thoughts about the past are inside a large balloon. The wind is picking up and you are holding the string to the balloon. The balloon, with those past jealousies, is lifting you off the ground. But you don't want to get pulled up in the air and carried away.

As you are lifted off the ground, you let the string go. The balloon with all those jealousies drifts into the air above, turns in the wind, and drifts off—farther away from you. As you watch, you feel freed. The past drifts away, and you are here—in the present moment—with your feet firmly planted on the ground. Letting go allows you to take the next step.

Let go of the balloon.

You Can Only Have a Relationship Today

How often do you and your partner get stuck in arguments about the past? You bring up your partner's past behavior, even behavior before you met each other, as if you are litigating his or her guilt. You bring up all kinds of past behaviors, past injuries, past suspicions. And then you dwell on them, argue with your partner, worry about what it all means, and fail to realize that you have just missed an opportunity to live in the present moment. It's like going to your favorite restaurant, asking for a table, spending the next hour complaining about a meal that you didn't like two years ago, and never ordering anything. You then walk out and wonder why you are still hungry.

What happened before your relationship began is simply *information*. It may not be information that has any relevance to how you treat each other in the present moment. No one will say, "We have a great relationship because we spend a lot of time talking about how upset I am with what she did before she met me." Good relationships are based on how rewarding, trusting, and accepting we are in the present moment. *Relationships are now.*

The past is always with us, but only in the present moment can you love your partner and feel loved. You can only enjoy life by living it right now. Because every moment comes and goes.

Chapter 12

"It's Complicated"— Getting Past Infidelity

Sometimes jealousy is totally justified. It represents a healthy and self-affirming response to a violation of trust. In this chapter, you will gain options you can examine when your partner has been unfaithful. You can consider your relationship and what your next move will be.

Keep in mind that whether your partner has been faithful or unfaithful, you still need to live your life. Getting hijacked by your jealousy, ruminating, feeling stuck, raging against what has happened, and feeling humiliated, defeated, and hopeless will not work in your favor. Even after experiencing a betrayal, you can learn how to cope better and, maybe, if both of you are willing to do the work, save your relationship. These will be your choices— just keep in mind that you do have choices. Let's look at an example of a woman who was experiencing jealousy about her husband's behavior.

> Alice was suspicious of Paul's relationship with Linda, who worked in his office. Alice thought their relationship was more than just professional. When I met with Paul, he told me that Alice's suspicions were unjustified and that he valued Linda as a friend. Linda had left his office and was working somewhere else. But as Paul began to trust

me more, he admitted that he had been sexually involved with Linda a few times. Paul told me that his relationship with Alice had grown further apart and that he felt they had little in common anymore. After the kids left the house, he realized his communication and intimacy with Alice had deteriorated, so he sought those things from Linda. Alice continued to confront him, and when she finally found a text message on his phone, Paul confessed his affair. Alice was infuriated and depressed, and said that she couldn't imagine how they could go on together.

As difficult as this was, it turned out not to be the end of their marriage. As they worked together in both couple and individual therapy, we decided on some ground rules that they would have to agree to. First, they agreed that Paul could no longer see or contact Linda—who was working somewhere else. This included no text messages, phone calls, or meetings. Second, he had to tell Linda that it was over with her and that he was committed to working on his marriage. Third, they both had to identify the kind of relationship they wanted to have in the future. This included the communication that they wanted, activities that they could share, and ways of reinforcing and respecting each other. Fourth, they had to develop a plan about how they would collaborate to work on solving problems together: no more blaming, no more withdrawing or stonewalling, and no more dismissing each other.

In this chapter, we will discuss what happens after an infidelity has been discovered because jealousy is most intense when we have been betrayed. When trust has been broken, it triggers a number of thoughts that we might have about ourselves, other people, and future relationships. So we will examine what those thoughts and feelings might be and how to cope with them. Because this crisis can be a possible turning point, we will look at ways to open doors to either getting out of the relationship, if that is what you decide, or choosing to make the relationship better.

You will see that trust, once broken, is difficult to regain—but it's not impossible. You and your partner might have mixed feelings about working on regaining trust. But you can still work together to move things forward, while acknowledging that distrust is still lurking within you. Let's take a look at the options when trust has been broken.

A Crisis Can Be a Turning Point

An affair that is discovered is one of the leading causes of divorce. Regaining trust is difficult, sometimes seemingly impossible, and many couples decide that an affair is the straw that finally broke the camel's back, because affairs don't arise out of nowhere. They happen because relationships have deteriorated, communication has fallen apart, partners are sharing fewer activities together, and the value of the relationship has decreased for one partner or both partners. This is not meant to justify affairs, or to blame the partner who feels betrayed. Commitments are important and living up to commitments is essential. But people are imperfect, fallible, and troubled. Even good people go astray, good people let us down, and people who love us can still hurt us deeply.

I have seen couples break up after an affair is discovered and I have also seen couples build stronger relationships. There is no simple route to take. It's up to you to examine what has happened, what it means, and what you both are willing to do.

You can think about an affair that is discovered as a turning point. Will this provide you with enough motivation to finally break it off? Does this mean that the two of you, who may have been together for years, must finally separate? Perhaps it does, but it is not inevitable. It can also mean that both of you are now in a crisis, in which you finally recognize that there is too much at stake to walk away. After all the disappointments and betrayals, you both may finally have the motivation to rebuild your relationship.

The affair can mark a point in time in between two relationships: the relationship that led up to an affair and the relationship that you rebuild after the affair. You wouldn't want to go back to the relationship that led to an affair, would you? Perhaps it is an opportunity to start a new relationship—with your partner. If the relationship led to an affair, you should think about what was missing in that relationship—not to blame yourself or the other person—but to learn where things went wrong so you can examine how the two of you can fix it, if you think that's possible.

Get Clarity on Commitment Levels

Sometimes it may not be clear what each partner's level of commitment is.

> Wendy had been dating Larry for a couple of months and they had been sexually intimate. She assumed that they had an agreement about monogamy, but they never explicitly talked about it. When she found out that he was also seeing other women, she was enraged and felt betrayed. Her feelings are understandable because sexual intimacy is often equated with some kind of commitment. But this is not an assumption that everyone makes.

The first issue to clarify is what the two of you can agree on regarding other relationships. Some people think of their sexual partners as "friends with benefits," that is, sex partners without the commitment of fidelity. If you have entered an understanding like this, be honest with yourself about whether you are really able to compartmentalize in this way. Although some people agree on an "open relationship," in which both partners are able to be with others, I have seldom seen this work for very long. Usually it turns out that one person wants more monogamy, more commitment. So take an honest look at your feelings because, if you are feeling jealous, you may not be as sophisticated as you set out to be.

When talking about commitment, listen to what the other person says. If your current partner says he or she is not ready for a commitment, then listen to that, and don't expect a commitment simply because *you are ready for one*. And don't equate sexual intimacy with commitment.

Be direct with each other. Be clear about what commitment means to you. Does it mean that you don't date other people? Or that you don't have sex with other people? Does it mean that you see each other frequently? Some people might get frightened or turned off when you bring up the issue of commitment, and they say, "Stop pressuring me." If that is the response you get, then you might conclude that there is no real commitment of fidelity. Then you can evaluate your choices accordingly. You need to decide whether you want to continue a relationship in which the commitment is one-sided. What is not promised cannot be taken for granted.

Neither trying to lay a guilt trip on your partner, nor threatening him or her, will have much effect. Pressuring someone into a commitment can lead to an agreement in the moment, but the other person may not intend to follow it. Perhaps he or she simply needs more time to reach that point of commitment, so you need to decide whether you are willing to wait. You can always say, "I guess we are looking for different things," while accepting that continuing along will only demoralize you. It's your choice to stay or leave.

The Response to Infidelity

Let's assume that the two of you do have an agreed-upon commitment that includes fidelity. If you are dating and there is no long-term commitment, you can determine whether your partner is willing to work on building trust. One way to determine this is to observe how he or she responds to the infidelity being discovered.

- Does he blame you? "You never seem interested in sex or in spending time with me."

- Does she minimize the other relationship? "He meant nothing to me. It was one night."

- Does he label you as neurotic or insecure? "You are just jealous and insecure. Get over it."

- Does she act entitled to do whatever she wants to do? "You can't tell me what I can do and who I can see."

- Does he justify his behavior by claiming he was drunk or stressed out? "It meant nothing, I was drunk" or "I was going through a difficult time."

- Does she stonewall you and tell you that she is not going to talk about it? "I don't want to discuss this. It's just going to make us have a fight."

The problem with each of these dismissive responses is that they only add to your distrust and sense of marginalization. When people have done things that hurt us, the last thing we want is to be blamed, invalidated, and humiliated for their problematic behavior.

Here's what it sounds like when someone has the wrong response. Derek came to see me a few years ago. He was complaining that his wife kept nagging him about his sexual infidelity. He said to me, "I told her it didn't mean anything. I was drunk. She can't get over it." He asked me what he should say to her so that she "would get over it." I told Derek that dismissing his wife's feelings and justifying his behavior by claiming that he was drunk would only make her feel worse—and certainly would not build trust. His behavior was totally invalidating and self-serving. Here is some of our conversation.

Bob: Why don't you tell her that you acted like a jerk, that she has every right to be angry with you, and that you can only hope eventually she might forgive you. You can say you realize that you really don't deserve forgiveness, and that it is completely up to her.

Derek: (*Laughing*) You know, you're right, that's really what I need to say.

Bob: How would you feel if your wife had been unfaithful? How would you feel if she excused her behavior by claiming that she was drunk?

Derek: I'd be really pissed off. I can't imagine forgiving her.

Bob: Well, that's the dilemma you have. Because I know that you want to preserve your relationship with her, and I think that you actually love her, but you won't be able to work toward reconciling by excusing yourself and telling her to get over it. You can't act like you are entitled to forgiveness. It is really up to her.

There are more helpful ways for your partner to respond after a transgression. They include the following.

- Owning up to the fact that what he did was wrong

- Acknowledging sincerely that she is truly sorry for doing this

- Telling you that you deserved better treatment

- Expressing guilt or shame over what he did

- Being willing to talk to you about your feelings

- Promising to help build trust in the relationship

- Conveying her willingness to work on making the relationship better for both of you

What Does the Infidelity Mean to You?

When someone betrays you, it's natural to have doubts about yourself and about the future of the relationship. Look at some of these statements and see whether any of them might apply to you. Then we'll look more closely at each of them.

- My partner sought out someone else because I am no longer attractive

- The other person must have something that I don't have

- I look like a fool and people will think I am a loser

- I can never get over this

- I can never trust my partner again

- This means our entire relationship was a waste of time or a fraud

- I will never be able to trust anyone again

"My Partner Sought Out Someone Else Because I Am No Longer Attractive"

There are many reasons why someone is unfaithful, but I have found that this one is very rare. Much infidelity is driven by:

- Anger and tension between partners

- The sense of excitement in pursuing something new and forbidden

- A belief in getting away with it

- Boredom

- A desire for variety

- The belief that experiences can be compartmentalized

- An attempt to boost one's ego

- Lack of foresight about what the consequences might be

For example, one man who loved his wife and children complained that he would get bored during the afternoon in his office. He would go to a massage parlor for some "easy and simple sex" to get his mind off things. He thought this was relaxing. His wife found out and it precipitated extreme conflict in their marriage. We worked on better ways for him to handle his boredom, and better ways to keep the possible risks in mind.

Another man was motivated to have an affair by his sense of entitlement to having things his way and conflicts with his wife. It had nothing to do with how attractive his wife was sexually. In a sense, it was part of his passive-aggressive pattern, as well as his incorrect belief that he would never get caught. His girlfriend finally called his wife and things exploded at home—much to his surprise.

"The Other Person Must Have Something That I Don't Have"

What could that other person have that you don't? Perhaps it was novelty, pursuing the forbidden, excitement, or variety. Or the attraction might have been that your partner felt less threatened, less obligated, or more able to talk about things with the other person. One man who had a long affair with another woman said, "I would never leave my wife for her, this was just something on the side."

Sometimes people do leave their spouses for the other person. But I have observed that affairs seldom lead to a new marriage. Affairs seem to be more about excitement, novelty, and hedging bets. As one man said, "I don't have to rely on my wife so much with someone on the side." Of course, he changed his mind when the girlfriend contacted his wife.

"I Look Like A Fool And People Will Think I Am A Loser"

Now, just think about this for a minute. Someone has lied to you and cheated on you, and now you think this means you look like a fool? My experience is that other people are much more likely to judge the person who betrayed you and, if anything, have compassion for you and even defend you. The person who betrayed you was the one who broke the trust, not you. If you are concerned that people might judge you harshly because your partner cheated on you, then think about whether these are true friends. And ask yourself whether you would judge anyone harshly if they were cheated on. What feelings do you have toward people who were betrayed? Would you be angry with them or would you feel compassion for them? Would you comfort them or would you criticize them?

"I Can Never Get Over This"

The shock of discovering infidelity may make you feel extremely angry, depressed, confused, and hopeless. These are powerful feelings that may be the lens through which you look at your future. But like almost any emotion that we have, these emotions eventually become less intense. We often project our future emotions based on how we feel at the present time.

Think back about a past instance when you had an intense, negative emotion. You may have experienced an extreme loss in your life, like the death of someone close to you, or a disappointment such as losing a job, or feeling betrayed by a friend or former lover. Now fast-forward from that past experience to the present and you will realize that, for much of the time in between the past intense feelings and the present ones, these strong negative feelings had eroded. In fact, you will probably be able to recall some very pleasant emotions and experiences that occurred during the interim. While you may naturally think you will never get over this—and it is important to validate how painful that thought is—we tend to be more resilient than we think we are. We tend to be stronger than we might feel in the moment when a crisis is occurring.

"I Can Never Trust My Partner Again"

Again, this is a very natural response on your part and one that almost anyone would have after experiencing a betrayal. But it could also be that you might eventually view this transgression in the context of the larger aspects of your intimate relationship. For example, one man told me that his wife had an intimate relationship with another man when he and his wife were going through a particularly difficult time. However, as they worked on the relationship, partnered up to take care of their children, and got on with their day-to-day lives, the wife's betrayal became less important to him. I am not saying that you should be indifferent or just bounce back. I am suggesting that you might look at the entire context of your relationship—your past, your present, and your possible future.

It will not be easy to rebuild trust after an infidelity has been discovered. It's not going to happen just by making a promise, apologizing, or simply wanting things to change. Both of you may have mixed motivations about rebuilding trust, including your fear of getting hurt again or your partner's resistance to having his or her behavior curtailed and controlled. I suggest thinking about developing a plan to rebuild trust. It won't just happen on its own.

"This Means Our Entire Relationship Was a Waste of Time or a Fraud"

This kind of all-or-nothing thinking often occurs when we are angry or anxious. And this may make you feel despondent and humiliated. It may lead you to believe anything that seemed good in the relationship in the past was a fraud. But this would not be a reasonable or an accurate way of looking at it. After all, there were many positive experiences that you can probably recall just reading this sentence at the present time. You may then respond, "But thinking about those positives only makes me feel worse." Yes, that may be true. In fact, you might want to convince yourself that the relationship was meaningless and that you're not losing anything. But again, you may want to step back to think about the other positives in the relationship. Consider whether those positives could be regained and strengthened in the future. That way, the betrayal can be put into the context of a relationship that can grow after the injury you have experienced.

"I Will Never Be Able to Trust Anyone Again"

When one woman found out about her husband's affair with a woman at work, she felt devastated and humiliated. She told me, "I'll never be able to trust anyone again." As she worked through the difficulties of the divorce and custody issues, she realized that she had a lot of things going for her as a person. She also realized that she would want to have a relationship with another man again—just not the man she was divorcing.

Her first response after the betrayal, that she could never trust anyone again, was a self-protective response. She was trying to protect herself from future betrayal. However, she realized that her desires to have companionship, share her life, and learn from the past relationship were more important than her fear of being hurt. I said to her, "If you don't get involved with someone, you'll feel hurt. And if you do get involved with someone, you might get hurt. We can't go through life expecting that bad things won't happen to us. The question to ask yourself is: *Is it worth it?*"

Three years later, she came back to see me to discuss her son. She told me she was relieved that her previous marriage had ended. For the past year, she had been involved with another man, who was a more equal partner. She realized that the betrayal that led to the divorce had opened a door in her life. It led her to a new relationship and greater personal growth. She felt that she could trust again because she was with a man who was trustworthy, and who shared a lot of the same interests and values. So keep in mind that your belief that you will never trust again, or love again, may be your first response to betrayal. But your first response may not be the response that you have in the future. You will have to see what happens in your life.

Developing Motivation to Change

After the infidelity has been discovered, the two of you may want to consider developing a plan to rebuild trust. Trust is not something that occurs simply because you want it. You can't simply rely on affirmations, promises, and apologies. Trust is like a muscle that may have weakened or atrophied over time, and it may require a lot of work to rebuild it—with no guarantees that the work will pay off. And it's not simply one person doing the work. It's something that you must work on together.

I want to start with a question that may seem unnecessary to you. That question is, "What are the advantages of rebuilding trust and what are the disadvantages of rebuilding trust?" You and your partner might talk about the pros and cons.

Advantages to Rebuilding Trust

- You feel less anxious

- You feel closer to each other

- You are able to plan the future without worrying about what might happen

It might feel nice to have regained trust, but let's not be naïve about this. Don't be blithe about a betrayal. I recognize how significant that can be for anyone. We don't know yet how your trust can be regained in the relationship. So it may be something that you need a wait-and-see attitude about. And waiting may be painful.

Disadvantages to Rebuilding Trust

You might think, "If I was betrayed once, I would be a fool to allow myself to trust that person again." This is a perfectly legitimate response and something that you might want to consider. If you were the one who was betrayed, you are going to think that you don't want to make yourself vulnerable again. However, you might balance this against your desire to continue—and even improve—the relationship.

If you are the one who engaged in the infidelity, then you need to think about what compromises and changes you are willing to make to rebuild trust. You can't simply say to your partner, "I am sorry I did what I did, so trust me again." You may sincerely believe what you are saying, but that's not going to be very convincing. Trust is something that is regained by *proven actions*, which means that you may have to make some changes that you will not like. So to regain trust, you need to both work on it and be honest about your mixed feelings about working on it.

Some people say, "How can I work on a relationship if I distrust my partner?" This is a perfectly legitimate and natural thought. But the two things are not mutually exclusive. You can work on better communication, more rewarding experiences for the two of you, solving problems together, setting positive goals that you work on, while simultaneously acknowledging your lack of total trust. By accepting that *for now you are distrustful*, you can carry this along with you while you work at rebuilding the positive things in your relationship.

Developing Ground Rules

Let's assume for a moment you have decided that you want to rebuild trust. This may mean that you need to develop some ground rules about what you share and describe to each other. For example, one man told me he would have secret meetings, lunches, dinners, and drinks with his former girlfriends—without telling the woman he was living with about these side adventures. He claimed that the girlfriends were still friends of his, and that these meetings really meant nothing about his current relationship. However, his live-in partner, who wanted to get married and have a child with him, felt betrayed when she found out about one of his secret meetings.

They decided that they would establish this ground rule: no future secretive meetings. He would disclose any plan to meet an ex-girlfriend or friend, and he would describe the whole event to her. Initially he was resistant because he wanted to keep his options open, enjoyed the flirtations, and also viewed himself as independent. He did not like the idea of having to answer to anyone. I suggested to him that if he was going to be part of a *couple*, then he could not simply think like an individual who was a completely free agent. He needed to think about how his behavior would be viewed, in terms of trust. If he was hiding these meetings from his partner, then he was being secretive, which would erode any trust. I offered my observation that many people think that they can compartmentalize their lives, have secret rendezvous with other people, and keep this separate from their primary relationship. But doing this causes a great deal of stress in the long term, and often eventually ends in a major crisis when these side adventures are discovered by the primary partner.

My recommendation was: *keep things simple*. I suggested that while the temptation to have these flirtatious meetings might yield short-term gratification for an hour or so of pleasure, and some short-term ego boosting, the long-term costs might be more long-lasting and severe. He would need to weigh the pleasure of the flirtation against the risk of hurting his partner and endangering his relationship. The question was: "Is it worth it?"

Trust is something that requires time and work—it is built slowly. Improving through communication, positive experiences, and shared activities helps build trust. But it will not happen overnight.

And trust is something that needs to be *protected*. I ask people, "What are you going to do today to protect the trust that you and your partner have with each other?" When we look at the relationship as *our thing* rather than *what I want at the moment*, we build trust. This is because by making decisions based on what is good for the relationship, and not simply on the basis of what I want or what is good for me in the present moment, we can rebuild trust and a relationship. Thinking about the relationship as valued and something that you want to protect is the best way to preserve it. When building trust, you might think, "How will this action or this decision affect how my partner will feel or how she will trust me?" Trust is a *goal*, not simply an accidental consequence that you hope occurs. Trust doesn't just happen.

Listening to Your Partner

If you do want your partner to tell you about what they are doing, or planning on doing, you also need to think about how you respond to them. For example, if you want your partner to tell you about people that he interacts with in the office, or at social gatherings, you need to be willing to listen to what he says without attacking him.

> Roger was very jealous of Sandra's business associates and he would question her about her interactions with them. She was understandably defensive and did not want to be interrogated. In the course of a number of months of

arguments, she finally did disclose that on a business trip she had gotten drunk and had been sexually intimate with one of her business associates. This enraged and demoralized Roger. Roger told me that this proved that he was completely right about his jealousy.

Understandably, Roger grew even more jealous and anxious after the betrayal was disclosed. However, this turned out to be a turning point in the relationship. Sandra told him that she was going through a midlife crisis, that she felt she was becoming less attractive, and that her self-esteem had declined in recent months. Over the prior year, with all the arguments and interrogations with Roger, she had become more distant from him. She said she knew that what she did was wrong, she felt very guilty, and she felt bad about letting Roger down because he deserved better treatment. So rather than break up, they used this as the turning point—the crisis that would open a new door. They decided to work on the relationship and rebuild some of the qualities that had brought them together in the first place. They loved their children, they also enjoyed doing things together, and both of them realized that their sexual relationship needed to be renewed and restored.

I discussed with Roger that, if he and Sandra were going to rebuild trust, then he would need to respond to her in a different way when she disclosed interactions with business associates. After all, she was in the business world, so her life involved travel and a lot of male coworkers. If he wanted Sandra to tell him that a man had been flirtatious, or that she had met with a man for a business meeting, he would be wise not to attack her or become hostile toward her when she was simply disclosing things that she was doing as part of her work. I also indicated to him that just as he felt his wife was attractive, other men would also think of her that way. It might be natural to expect that they will try to flirt with her—but it didn't mean that she was going to be unfaithful. Because he wanted her to trust him and tell him about her interactions, he needed to listen more patiently to what she said. He would have to listen if he wanted her to talk.

Listening respectfully to your partner does not mean that you don't feel jealous while you are listening. You can have a feeling without accusing your partner or attacking them. Your feelings can be experiences *inside you*. You can also come to an agreement with your partner where you can say, "When you tell me about this, I feel jealous," without accusing your partner of wrongdoing. The two of you decide what behaviors are acceptable—but if you want your partner to talk to you about what he or she is doing, you must listen in a manner that is respectful. Trust works both ways, for the one talking and the one listening.

Focus on Common Goals

One way of building trust is to focus on common goals. Rather than focusing on the conflict or the betrayal (which you will be thinking about, no matter what), you can focus on specific values and goals that you share. This can include being good parents, making plans together, and sharing activities. Start to think of yourselves as a *team of two* rather than thinking of yourselves as adversaries.

I remember one couple who focused on what they disagreed about, and then would argue and defend themselves to no avail. I suggested that they identify some common goals—even if they just thought up some simple activities. I asked the wife and husband to write down some activities that each would like to share with the other. When they had finished their individual lists, I wrote both on the blackboard. Of course there were some activities that they did not share a common interest in (like watching football games on TV), but there were some activities that they would be willing to share. So they negotiated *common ground*. They started by planning to act on some of these common goals, and then to see how things went. Much to their surprise, they had a lot in common once they could agree that they could accept what they did not have in common.

Another couple who had gone through the crisis of infidelity realized that they had the welfare of their three children in common. So I suggested that we work on what they could agree on to make the lives of their children better. They discussed making agreements about discipline, rewards, study time, and playdates with other kids. They discussed plans for summer camp and which camp would be best for their daughters. We eventually focused on the kinds of values and traits that they wanted their daughters to have—such as compassion, kindness, self-control, integrity, and cooperativeness. This then led to a discussion of how they could both model these qualities for their children. As they recognized and worked toward a common goal, they began to build more trust for each other, recognizing that they needed each other to be better parents. By sharing values and goals, they began to move beyond the disappointments and resentments of the past.

This final chapter could have made up the contents of a book alone, but that would be far beyond the scope of what this book is about—*jealousy*. My purpose has been to demonstrate that jealousy is sometimes a justified and healthy response, and may be an adaptive first response to the violation of trust. But we can also think of jealousy as the first step in a longer process of developing motivation to change your relationship, ground rules for building trust, skills for being a better listener, a view of the relationship as *our thing* rather than *my way*, and a bond through common goals and values. It would be naïve to think that this process will be easy, but it is not impossible. Only you and your partner can determine what is possible for both of you and it might require a lot of patience and difficult work to come to that realization.

Concluding Reflections

This book may seem like a long journey into the emotional recesses of jealousy. Rather than viewing jealousy in simplistic terms, as low self-esteem or unrealistic demands, I have chosen to explore with you the universality of jealousy—in infants, animals, and throughout history—and to describe its evolutionary adaptiveness. Jealousy is related to "parental investment" and protecting our interests in passing on our genes. It is related to the natural tendency to protect our interests with family, friends, and colleagues. As Saint Augustine observed, "He who is without jealousy has never loved." It is the emotion that can plague you, drive friends apart, and disintegrate families. It is the stuff of songs, sagas, tragedies, and poems.

It is a strong, and sometimes dangerous, emotion that deserves respectful consideration. My hope is that you can see that you are not alone in your jealousy. You can also understand that it is important to validate the difficulty of experiencing jealousy because it reflects painful, and often confusing, emotions of love, fear, and even hate about the person most central in your life. Part of this validation is directing compassion toward yourself while experiencing the storm of jealous emotions and, where possible, feeling compassion toward your partner. This is understandably difficult and may feel impossible at times, but it is something to think about, aim for, and even struggle to embrace.

You have learned about the difference between the thoughts underlying jealousy ("My partner is interested in her") and the feelings that result from these thoughts (anger, anxiety, resentment). And you have learned that it is possible to have jealous thoughts and feelings, but choose whether you take action. Sometimes realizing that you can have a feeling, but still have a choice, can be liberating. You don't have to hold on to the rope that pulls you in another direction.

We have seen that, once the mind and heart are hijacked by jealousy, you may find yourself overwhelmed with the feelings—and then act in ways that you hope will end your pain. But the actions that we take when we feel jealous may be more detrimental to our interests than the feelings we experience. These actions, which I view as strategies, comprise a wide range of behaviors that we think will control what is happening and put an end to our torment. They include interrogating, checking, looking for clues, reassurance-seeking, spying, stalking, undermining the confidence of our partners, threatening to leave, and withdrawing. As much as these strategies may seem to make sense emotionally at the time of intense feeling, each of them carries the risk of perpetuating what we most fear—the dissolution of the relationship. Perhaps there are better ways.

Certainly all of us have a right to our feelings, and feeling jealous is so widespread that you will realize that you are not alone. The issue to work with is how the Jealousy Hijack results in rumination, worry, depression, and intense relationship conflict. It's more about how to moderate the consequences of the feelings. We have seen that it might be helpful—although difficult—to step back from the jealous thoughts and feelings, while accepting that you have these experiences. Stepping back can allow us to make room for the feelings, to live alongside of what we think and feel, without being controlled by our experiences. This mindful detachment and acceptance doesn't mean that we are saying it is okay that partners may or may not be doing what we suspect. Rather, it means that we acknowledge thoughts and feelings, without taking the actions that might jeopardize our interests.

When we step back, we can also momentarily reflect on the reasonableness and rationality of what we are thinking. As we are often hijacked by mindreading what our partner desires or fortunetelling a disastrous outcome, we can evaluate whether the evidence really supports what our thoughts seem to tell us. Sometimes we are biased and focused on a particular way of seeing things—and sometimes we may be right. But the intensity of our emotion is no indication of the validity of our beliefs. It may be worth standing back and evaluating. We often don't really know what the facts are.

We have also seen that we may have rules and assumptions that feed our jealousy, which are often based on perfectionistic beliefs about love, commitment, and relationships. Some of this may reflect a view that our partner should never find someone attractive, or the belief that the past our partner had is a threat to the present. Driven by these perfectionistic beliefs, we often suffer more than we need to. Reality is not based on purity or perfection; it reflects that we are all fallen angels, all in need of improvement, all seeking understanding and—if necessary—forgiveness. Everyone has a past, including you, but it is the present and future that will matter most.

When we talk to our partners about our jealousy, we need to keep in mind that both of us want to feel respected, both of us want to feel trusted. It's natural to want to lash out with rage, labels, and accusations—and it may be that our partner has fallen short, is hiding something, or has betrayed our trust. But it also may be the case that respectful discussion about different views of what is happening may help clarify guidelines for building trust in the future.

As you may realize, now that you have read through this book, there are many ways to look at your jealous thoughts, feelings, and behaviors. There are many metaphors that you can use and responses that you can have. There is no one-size-fits-all program for handling jealousy, because you are unique and your relationship is unique—and always in flow. We often hope when we get involved in a new relationship that it will be perfect, there won't be any roadblocks, detours, or head-on collisions, but life that is fully lived is also filled with disappointments. We are all fallen angels at times.

None of us is without fault, without need for growth. All relationships, it seems, are filled with unfinished business. I like the metaphor of the relationship room, which is where we can imagine both partners living in a crowded room, filled with memories and an ever-changing landscape. It is *your room, together.* Making room for the jealousy can allow the two of you to live together. You don't always have to walk out the door.

Acknowledgments

This book owes a lot to many people, none of whom should be held responsible for any shortcomings on my part. I want to first thank my editor, Ryan Buresh from New Harbinger Publications, who has been a strong advocate and an excellent source of feedback for structuring the book to make it more readable and helpful. Matthew McKay of New Harbinger has graciously welcomed me into their fold and I am grateful for his support—and for his sense of humor. In addition, my other editors at New Harbinger, Clancy Drake, Caleb Beckwith, and Vicraj Gill, gave a great deal of attention to the details and final product, and I thank them for their careful work. My research assistant, Sindhu Shivaji, worked long hours helping with research and editing, and I thank her and wish her well as she moves on in her career in psychology. Bob Diforio, my "bulldog" agent, has always been a great source of support and a wonderful advocate, and I am deeply indebted to him.

There are numerous people whose work I value and learned from. I wish to acknowledge the following scholars whose work has been of value to me: David Buss, David A. Clark, David M. Clark, Paul Gilbert, Steve Hayes, Stefan Hofmann, Marsha M. Linehan, Zindel V. Segal, Dennis Tirch, Adrian Wells, and Mark Williams. My colleagues at The American Institute for Cognitive Therapy (http://www.cognitivetherapynyc.com) have been a wonderful source of support and ideas and have listened to various parts of this book in different degrees of development. Thank you for your patience.

And, as always, I am forever blessed to have Helen as my loving wife. I am continually fascinated by her ability to accept what is less than perfect in me. It is to her and her open heart that this book is dedicated.

Notes

1. D. M. Buss, *Dangerous Passion* (New York: Free Press, 2000).

2. R. L. Leahy, *Emotional Schema Therapy* (New York: Guilford Press, 2015).

3. C. Darwin, *The Descent of Man and Selection in Relation to Sex* (London: John Murray, 1871).

4. R. L. Trivers, "Parental Investment and Sexual Selection," in *Sexual Selection and the Descent of Man, 1871–1971* (Chicago: Aldine, 1972), 136–79.

5. D. C. Geary, M. Rumsey, C. Bow-Thomas, and M. K. Hoard, "Sexual Jealousy as a Facultative Trait: Evidence from the Pattern of Sex Differences in Adults from China and the United States," *Ethology and Sociobiology* 16, no. 5 (1995): 355–83.

6. Ibid.; B. P. Buunk, A. Angleitner, V. Oubaid, and D. M. Buss, "Sex Differences in Jealousy in Evolutionary and Cultural Perspective: Tests from the Netherlands, Germany, and the United States," *Psychological Science* 7, no. 6 (1996): 359–63.

7. S. Hart and H. Carrington, "Jealousy in 6-Month-Old Infants," *Infancy* 3, no. 3 (2002): 395–402; S. Hart, T. Field, C. Del Valle, and M. Letourneau, "Infants Protest Their Mothers' Attending to an Infant-Size Doll," *Social Development* 7, no. 1 (1998): 54–61.

8. P. H. Morris, C. D. Doe, and E. Godsell, "Secondary Emotions in Non-Primate Species? Behavioral Reports and Subjective Claims by Animal Owners," *Cognition and Emotion* 22, no. 1 (2008): 3–20.

9. Exodus 20:5 (King James).

10. C. Andreas and J. J. Parry, *The Art of Courtly Love* (New York: Columbia University Press, 1990), 1186.

11. W. Shakespeare, *Othello*, 5.2.

12. P. N. Stearns, *American Cool: Constructing a Twentieth-Century Emotional Style* (New York: NYU Press, 1994).

13. B. R. Karney, C. Wilson, and M. S. Thomas, *Family Formation in Florida: 2003 Baseline Survey of Attitudes, Beliefs, and Demographics Relating to Marriage and Family Formation* (Gainesville, FL: University of Florida, 2003).

14. See http://www.childlessstepmums.co.uk.

15. Q. Fottrell, "Typical U.S. Worker Has Been 4.2 Years in Their Current Job," *Market Watch*, January 12, 2014. http://www.marketwatch.com/story/americans-less-likely-to-change-jobs-now-than-in-1980s-2014–01–10.

16. J. Bowlby, *Attachment and Loss*, vol. 1 *Attachment* (London: Hogarth, 1968).

17. M. Mikulincer and P. R. Shaver, "Attachment Theory and Intergroup Bias: Evidence That Priming the Secure Base Schema Attenuates Negative Reactions to Out-Groups," *Journal of Personality and Social Psychology* 81, no. 1 (2001): 97–115.

18. N. L. Collins, "Working Models of Attachment: Implications for Explanation, Emotion, and Behavior," *Journal of Personality and Social Psychology* 71, no. 4 (1996): 810.

19. B. P. Buunk, "Personality, Birth Order, and Attachment Styles as Related to Various Types of Jealousy," *Personality and Individual Differences* 23, no. 6 (1997): 997–1006; A. Holtzworth-Munroe, G. L. Stuart, and G. Hutchinson, "Violent Versus Nonviolent Husbands: Differences in Attachment Patterns, Dependency, and Jealousy," *Journal of Family Psychology* 11, no. 3 (1997): 314.

20. B. P. Buunk, "Personality, Birth Order, and Attachment Styles."

21. G. L. White, "Inducing Jealousy: A Power Perspective," *Personality and Social Psychology Bulletin* 6 (1980): 222–7; G. L. White, "A Model of Romantic Jealousy," *Motivation and Emotion* 5 (1981): 295–310; G. L. White and P. E. Mullen, *Jealousy: Theory, Research, and Clinical Strategies* (New York: Guilford Press, 1989).

22. L. Khanchandani and T. W. Durham, "Jealousy During Dating Among Female College Students," *College Student Journal* 43, no. 4 (2009): 1272.

23. M. J. Dugas, K. Buhr, and R. Ladouceur, "The Role of Intolerance of Uncertainty in the Etiology and Maintenance of Generalized Anxiety Disorder," in *Generalized Anxiety Disorder: Advances in Research and Practice* (New York: Guilford Press, 2004): 143–63.

24. J. L. Bevan and K. D. Tidgewell, "Relational Uncertainty as a Consequence of Partner Jealousy Expressions," *Communication Studies* 60, no. 3 (2009): 305–23.

25. Leahy, *Emotional Schema Therapy.*

26. R. L. Leahy, *Cognitive Therapy Techniques*, Second Edition (New York: Guilford Press, 2017).

27. R. L. Leahy, *The Worry Cure* (New York: Harmony Books, 2005).

28. A. Wells, *Metacognitive Therapy for Anxiety and Depression* (New York: Guilford Press, 2009).

29. R. L. Leahy and D. Tirch, "Cognitive Behavioral Therapy for Jealousy," *International Journal of Cognitive Therapy* 1 (2008): 18–32.

30. M. J. Dugas, et al., "Role of Intolerance of Uncertainty."

31. A. Wells, "A Cognitive Model of GAD: Metacognitions and Pathological Worry," in *Generalized Anxiety Disorder* (New York: Guilford Press, 2004), 164–86.

32. R. L. Leahy, *Beat the Blues Before They Beat You* (New York: Hay House, 2010).

33. Leahy, *Emotional Schema Therapy*.

34. Ibid.

35. S. C. Hayes, K. D. Strosahl, and K. G. Wilson, *Acceptance and Commitment Therapy* (New York: Guilford Press, 2011); E. Roemer and S. M. Orsillo, *Mindfulness and Acceptance-Based Behavior Therapies in Practice* (New York: Guilford Press, 2009); Leahy, *Emotional Schema Therapy*.

36. W. Whitman, "Song of Myself," *Leaves of Grass* (1892).

37. Leahy, *Emotional Schema Therapy*.

38. J. D. Teasdale and Z. V. Segal, *The Mindful Way Through Depression* (New York: Guilford Press, 2007).

39. P. Gilbert, *The Compassionate Mind* (London: Constable, 2009); D. Tirch, *The Compassionate-Mind Guide to Overcoming Anxiety* (Oakland, CA: New Harbinger, 2012).

40. Leahy, *The Worry Cure*; Wells, "A Cognitive Model of GAD."

41. Wells, *Metacognitive Therapy for Anxiety and Depression*.

42. Ibid.

43. Ibid.

44. Leahy, *The Worry Cure; Cognitive Therapy Techniques.*

45. Ibid.

46. R. J. Rydell, A. R. McConnell, and R. G. Bringle, "Jealousy and Commitment: Perceived Threat and the Effect of Relationship Alternatives," *Personal Relationships* 11 (2004): 451–68.

47. Gilbert, *The Compassionate Mind.*

48. TV Tropes, accessed July 17, 2017, http://tvtropes.org/pmwiki /pmwiki.php/Creator/RonWhite.

Robert L. Leahy, PhD, is author or editor of twenty-six books, including *The Worry Cure*. He has led or been heavily involved with many national and regional cognitive behavioral therapy (CBT) organizations. He writes a regular blog for *Psychology Today*, and has written for *The Huffington Post*. Leahy is an international speaker at conferences worldwide, and has been featured in print, radio, and television media such as *The New York Times*, *The Wall Street Journal*, *The Times of London*, *The Washington Post*, *20/20*, *The Early Show*, and more.

Foreword writer **Paul Gilbert, PhD**, is world renowned for his work on depression, shame, and self-criticism, and is developer of compassion-focused therapy (CFT). He is head of the mental health research unit at the University of Derby, and has authored or coauthored numerous scholarly articles and books, including *The Compassionate Mind*, *Mindful Compassion*, and *Overcoming Depression*.

MORE BOOKS *from*
NEW HARBINGER PUBLICATIONS

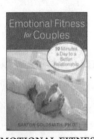

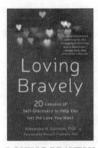